45 RPM

Published by
Princeton Architectural Press
37 East Seventh Street
New York, NY 10003

For a catalog of books published by Princeton Architectural Press, call toll free 800.722.6657 or visit www.papress.com.

04 03 02 5 4 3 2 1 First Edition

Printed in China

Editor: Mark Lamster
Design: Deb Wood/Spencer Drate/Yvette Awad
Research: Christiane Miller

Special thanks: Nettie Aljian, Ann Alter, Nicola Bednarek, Janet Behning, Penny Chu, Jan Cigliano, Russell Fernandez, Jan Haux, Clare Jacobson, Nancy Eklund Later, Linda Lee, Jane Sheinman, Katharine Smalley, Scott Tennent, and Jennifer Thompson of Princeton Architectural Press
—Kevin C. Lippert, publisher

Library of Congress Cataloging-in-Publication Data

45 RPM : a visual history of the seven-inch record / edited by Spencer Drate.
p. cm.
ISBN 1-56898-358-1 (alk. paper)
1. Sound recordings—Album covers. I. Title: Forty-five RPM. II. Drate, Spencer.
NC1882 .A15 2002
741.6'6—dc21
2002008638

45 RPM

A VISUAL HISTORY OF THE SEVEN-INCH RECORD
EDITED BY SPENCER DRATE

PRINCETON ARCHITECTURAL PRESS   NEW YORK

To Jütka, Justin, and Ariel, who bring music to my life.

THE BATTLE FOR THE VINYL FRONTIER

CHARLES L. GRANATA

"I VIGOROUSLY DECLARE THAT THE '45' IS HERE TO STAY, AND LET THERE BE NO DOUBT ABOUT IT!" —RCA VICTOR PRESIDENT FRANK FOLSOM, 1949

What is it about the 7-inch single that grabs our attention? Why does the format—long considered a dead medium—evoke sentimental memories nearly twenty years after its demise? And what is it that we see in the miniature cover art that has graced the 45 since its infancy in the early 1950s? The 45 was the "Gold Standard" of Top 40 radio play lists and king of the *Billboard* charts for more than thirty-five years before it was edged out of circulation by the compact disc in the early 1990s. It survives today as a symbol of the lofty times and lighthearted fun that popular music represented to postwar Americans. Nothing too serious—just Sinatra, Elvis, Chuck Berry, the Stones, and the Beatles served up on a handy format that was as much at home under the dashboard of a T-Bird as in the bedroom of an Eisenhower-era teenager.

Combining portability, clever design, and trend-setting music made for a brilliant marketing strategy. Within six months of its debut, the record industry was stamping out over a million 45-rpm platters per month, prompting RCA President Frank Folsom to proclaim that "the '45' system is destined to lead the phonograph field, both in players and in records." There is no better testament to the 45's integrity than the vigorous attention it still receives. More than fifty years after its debut, baby-boomer vinyl enthusiasts, serious record collectors, and "Gen-Xers" alike clamor to snap up original and EP "Extended Play" 45s on the second-hand record market.

It's not just the musical and historical significance that make these first-run pressings so desirable. The covers, beautifully printed on glossy paper sleeves and hard cardboard jackets, make them irresistibly appealing. On the new music scene, garage bands and independent labels churn out limited-edition singles and EPs (often on brightly colored wax reminiscent of the very first 45s issued by RCA Victor), the cover art usually exceeding the aesthetic value of the record's musical content.

The decades-long success of the 45-rpm single belies a turbulent history. In its infancy, the small disc was at the center of a fierce battle, a fight brimming with jealousy, greed, and caustic recriminations. The culmination saw two rival record companies emerge victorious, with the fallout of their erstwhile battle etched deeply into the vinyl landscape of twentieth-century pop music culture. The conflict (thereafter dubbed "The War of the Speeds") wasn't all for naught. From it sprang an irreplaceable fragment of Americana: the plastic 7-inch 45-rpm "single," a record product introduced by RCA Victor on 31 March 1949.

To fully appreciate the importance of the 45 and to understand the impact of its birth, we must trace the evolution of the modern "Long Play" LP record, perfected in 1948 by RCA's archrival, Columbia Records. Until 1948 records were made of a fragile shellac compound and rotated at a dizzying 78 revolutions per minute. Columbia's new LPs were 10-inch discs with a smooth plastic surface called Vinylite. These platters revolved at a much slower rate, 33-1/3 rpm, and in addition to a dramatic improvement in sound quality allowed for greater playing time. Columbia demonstrated the LP format during a press conference at New York's Waldorf Astoria hotel on 21 June 1948. Other than those involved in researching and developing the product, only one person knew of the impending announcement: RCA President General David Sarnoff, who was also head of RCA's parent company NBC. From all accounts, Sarnoff was not pleased.

"William Paley, the head of CBS, had invited him to a demonstration three weeks before," remembered Columbia executive Howard Scott. "RCA had plenty of time to move quickly and start doing their own transfers for LP, but they didn't. When Sarnoff heard the demonstration he was furious, and chewed out his entire staff in front of Paley and Columbia's Ted Wallerstein. He left in a huff, and of course it was two years before RCA would admit defeat and begin making 33-1/3-rpm records." Sarnoff's reaction was predictable. He was still harboring resentment over CBS's strides in

developing a color television system, something he had hoped NBC would perfect. Since RCA had developed one of the first LPs (a failed attempt that was made in 1931), Columbia's scoop was a serious blow to the company's pride.

As a rejoinder, RCA quickly developed and marketed a smaller microgroove disc revolving at 45 rpm, thereby touching off a skirmish in which three different formats and speeds (the 10-inch 78, 7-inch 45, and 10-inch 33-1/3) vied for position. Ultimately, the LP won out as the primary format for longer programming and the 45 replaced the 78 as the preferred choice for pop singles. In 1950 RCA finally gave up its fight against the CBS-engineered 33-1/3 record and began making its own LPs.

RCA's decision to use a speed of 45 rpm was based on calculations by Bell Laboratory scientist J. P. Maxfield. (The oft-repeated tale that a spiteful RCA executive arrived at the speed arbitrarily by subtracting 33 from 78 is erroneous.) After conducting extensive analysis of groove structure and associated problems for the Vitaphone Film Company in 1927, Maxfield concluded that the best compromise between adequate signal-to-noise ratio and playing time was three minutes per radial inch. "Calculus was used to show that the optimum use of a disc record of constant rotational speed occurs when the innermost recorded diameter is half the outermost recorded diameter," explained Peter Copeland of the British Library National Sound Archive. "That's why a 7-inch single has a label 3-1/2 inches in diameter."

Instead of a tiny spindle hole in its center, the 45 contained a donut-style opening requiring an adapter. Realizing that they'd need to compete with Columbia's long-play capability, RCA designed the disc to work on an automatic changer on which a pile of the discs could be stacked—an innovation that approximated Columbia's extended-play advantage.

At its Bridgeport, Connecticut laboratories, Columbia experimented with the smaller disc size, and in April 1949 introduced its own version of the single, the "Columbia Microgroove" record: a small-holed, 7-inch disc playing at 33-1/3 rpm. CBS didn't put much marketing into the product, and by early 1951 they had all but disappeared from record stores.

So what was the first 45-rpm single? *Whirl-Away Demonstration Record*, an RCA Victor marketing tool sent to record dealers when the new product debuted, was probably the first disc. Victor's first batch of releases was ambitious: seventy-six albums and 104 singles were issued simultaneously, flooding the market with a wide variety of music on the new format. Advance copies of RCA's initial cache of 45s were sent to record stores in February 1949, enclosed in a special envelope proclaiming, "This Is Your Preview of the New RCA Victor 45 R.P.M. RECORD LINE!"

"Use these seven records as samples between now and March 31st, and for use with the forthcoming window and counter displays," the RCA promotional literature trumpeted. Then, as an afterthought: "You may wish to hold them as collector's items—the first production run of a record that will set the pace for the entire industry!" Included in the kit was a sampling of discs reflecting the musical styles available on the Victor label. Each musical style had a place—and a color—in RCA's brilliant marketing plan. The promotional information was enthusiastic: "Sparkling identifying colors!—Record classification is simplified because a different color is used on the entire record . . . not just on the label to denote each classification. This helps you to determine the type of record at a mere glance."

In RCA's eyes, the color-coding system was appealing and fun. With minimal effort, buyers could instantly identify the area in which to find "their music," available in a rainbow of transparent colors: red for classical, midnight blue for light classics, green for country-western, yellow for children's music, sky blue for international, and cerise (orange) for R&B. Traditional black wax was reserved for the lucrative pop genre. The novelty of multicolor singles soon wore off, however, and by 1952 all of RCA Victor's discs were pressed in black, with colors reserved for special promotional pressings.

At first, single releases consisted of current pop hits, or reissues of existing 78-rpm recordings.

"Albums" were eight-song box sets configured to accommodate the label's highly touted automatic record changer. Where an ordinary pop single was labeled "Side 1" and "Side 2," the order for 45-rpm album sets was shuffled, so a whole album side could be stacked up on multiple 45s and replayed in their original LP sequencing. Thus, Side 1 was backed with Side 8, Side 2 with Side 7, Side 3 with Side 6, and Side 4 with Side 5. If the noisy 78s were a nuisance to listeners, the idea of a full symphony with repeated breaks for 45-rpm side changes was even more disconcerting—especially when they could hear the entire piece uninterrupted on one of Columbia's 12-inch LPs. For a time, RCA considered abandoning the 45-rpm format.

But by November 1949, kids across America were snapping up 45-rpm singles with gusto. "From coast to coast—teen-agers are lining up for bargain player attachments," boasted the *RCA Distributor's Record Bulletin* from 14 November 1949. "They go for the lowest priced at the new speed. They go for the little disc that fits on the shelf beside their paper-backed novels, is unbreakable, and has quality of tone that can't be matched." By the end of 1949, both Capitol and M-G-M Records had begun manufacturing the small discs, bringing their catalogs to a new, younger audience. Mercury and Decca followed in 1951. Of the major labels, Columbia was the last holdout, not commencing with production of 45s until late 1950, the same

year RCA relented and began manufacturing 12-inch LPs. As the popularity of the quiet, lightweight 45-rpm disc grew, the demand for old-fashioned, shellac 78-rpm records waned. By 1956 few labels were still pressing antiquated, noisy 78s. The 45 was here to stay.

Amusingly, the smaller format allowed for the integration of the vinyl phonograph record into automobiles. It was Columbia Records—RCA's "speed war" nemesis—that developed the first automotive phonographs in the mid-1950s. From 1956 to 1960, Chrysler offered an optional under-dash record player for their upscale models, such as the Plymouth Fury and the Chrysler New Yorker. "The Highway Hi-Fi" allowed for forty-five minutes of music pressed on custom-designed 16-rpm discs. At first, the repertoire consisted of classical performances and children's records from the Columbia catalog. The phonograph stylus and tone arm were housed inside an outer tone arm shell, so bumps and jolts wouldn't shake the stylus from its groove. Eventually, RCA joined the fray, offering an automotive model that played standard singles at 45 rpm, but it was an impractical system, requiring the driver to change discs every few minutes. By the early 1960s, the idea of playing records in the car had all but vanished, soon to be replaced by the wonders of the 8-track tape cartridge.

The speed war had a stimulating effect on the industry as a whole. Labels acquired "brand identities," and within a short time, were prominently touting patented sonic processes on the fronts of their sleeves. At RCA, the phrases "New Orthophonic High Fidelity" and "Living Stereo" were terms designed to denote superiority. Columbia heralded their "High Fidelity Plus" discs. At Capitol in Hollywood, they buzzed about "Full Dimensional Stereo." By the early 1950s, music executives recognized that incorporating first-rate graphics and design elements into their 10- and 12-inch LP jackets (and the sleeves and jackets of their 7-inch 45-rpm cousins) was a clever marketing strategy. Consequently, the labels engaged the services of such graphic artists as Jim Flora (RCA Victor), Alex Steinweiss (Columbia), and David Stone Martin (Norgran and Verve) to lend their record sleeves and covers a distinctive sensibility.

For some fifty years, the tradition of graphic excellence established by these innovators has made the 45 one of the most prized objects of fascination. From the simplicity of the four-song EP covers of the 1950s to the edgy, surreal art of the 1990s, every sleeve tells a story. The miniature jackets gracing the 45-rpm record add immeasurably to our enjoyment of the music *and* the medium, offering today's listener a total sensory experience that is lacking with the modern CD format. Using color, texture, and form, the artists and art directors responsible for drawing our attention to 45s approached their craft with style and substance.

The results, as illustrated by the many wonderful covers in this book, were sensational.

CHARLES L. GRANATA is a record producer, music historian, and the author of *Sessions with Sinatra: Frank Sinatra and the Art of Recording* (Acapella, 1999) and *You Still Believe In Me: Brian Wilson and the Making of Pet Sounds* (Unanimous, 2002).

HIPSTERS, LONGHAIRS, AND THE WAR ON SPEEDS

ERIC KOHLER

It would take most of the 1950s for the 45 to find its place as an icon of popular music—a position it held until the advent of the compact disc in the 1980s. With the invention of both the 45 and the LP, the public of the 1950s could buy an album from the major labels in all three speeds: 78, 33, or 45. This was the only decade in which every type of music could be found on 45s—even classical, though a symphony might require an album of fifteen 45s (as opposed to two LPs). It did not take long for the public to figure out that the little disc was ideally suited to the pop single. If an album of fifteen 45s was impractical for a symphony, a twelve-song LP was equally absurd on a jukebox. The 45 had finally found its place.

Because all genres of music were available on 45s during the 1950s, 45 album cover art was the most varied it would ever be. Many covers were just smaller versions of LP editions, but there were also covers created especially for the growing singles market. With the recent advance of marketing concepts in the recording industry, a hit single would now warrant a special cover that would entice the consumer and let them know they were buying a genuine "hit." The graphics for these were usually hard sell—large tabloid typography and silhouetted black-and-white photos of the artist.

The covers selected for this chapter represent a history in miniature of graphic design in the 1950s. Many feature design elements now identified with this period—the vertical stripes and typography of *Rosemary Clooney*, the use of the typeface Latin Wide on covers for Al Cohn, Matt Dennis, and Joni James, and the illustration style of Frank Sinatra's *Wee Small Hours*. Humor is another characteristic element in these covers; what some lack in high design aesthetics, they make up for in a charming naivete. *Les Paul and Mary Ford,* with its silhouetted photo heads with cartoon bodies—recalling the animated graphics of many TV shows and commercials of the period—is a good example of this. On *Sinatra Sings Irving Berlin*, the giant swirling *S* with Sinatra's face floating in the center has no relevance to the music but is a humorous, attention-getting device that seems right out of the dream sequence in *Vertigo*.

Mood music was a 1950s phenomenon that helped popularize "glamorous" cover photography and, in doing so, caused illustration to fall out of favor by the end of the decade. The samples shown here reflect a trend that swept the advertising world in the 1950s and would appear in all types of printed design. The crushed silk background and woman's pose in the cover for *Sax in Silk*, for example, could have easily appeared in a Pepsi or Cadillac magazine ad of the time.

There are just as many covers here that surpass the nostalgic as truly great examples of album cover design. The symbolism of *Modern Sounds* conveys the dynamism of Be Bop in a creative, humorous way. The large eyeglasses, an homage to the fad that Dizzy Gillespie started when all Bop enthusiasts sported a pair of these, the two juxtaposed ovals (one for the face and one for the logo), and the contrast between the hard Futura type and the loose hand-lettered script all convey the feeling of the music in a graphic manner. Because the size of the 45 was much smaller than the LP, some of the more successful designs contain only large decorative typography to create a kind of billboard effect that jumps out at the viewer. Frank Sinatra's *Carousel* features only some elegant hand lettering, which is all that is required to make a successful cover.

Album cover design was becoming such a popular communication medium that it enticed fine artists and illustrators—including Pablo Picasso and Salvador Dali—to lend their work to projects. It also produced several influential designers who set a visual standard for the decade, most prominently David Stone Martin and Burt Goldblatt. In the 1950s, Martin worked exclusively for Norman Granz's jazz labels (Clef, Norgran, and Verve). *Oscar Peterson Plays Duke Ellington* is a fine example of his black-and-white illustration style on a colored wash background with his signature Copperplate typeset at cockeyed angles. Goldblatt worked in both illustration and photography, mixing both with strong typography for the jazz labels for whom he worked. *Stan Getz Plays* is an illustrative example that contrasts with his bold use of colored shapes and type. Rather than relying on established design schemes, these two artists initiated trends that still influence designers today and helped give the first decade of 45 album design a strong visual identity.

ERIC KOHLER is a New York–based graphic designer and collector who has created album covers for Columbia, Blue Note, and Capitol Records. He is the author of *In The Groove: Vintage Record Graphics, 1940–1960* (Chronicle, 1999).

ED 2424

HERE'S LOOKIN' AT YOU · SAMMY DAVIS, JR.

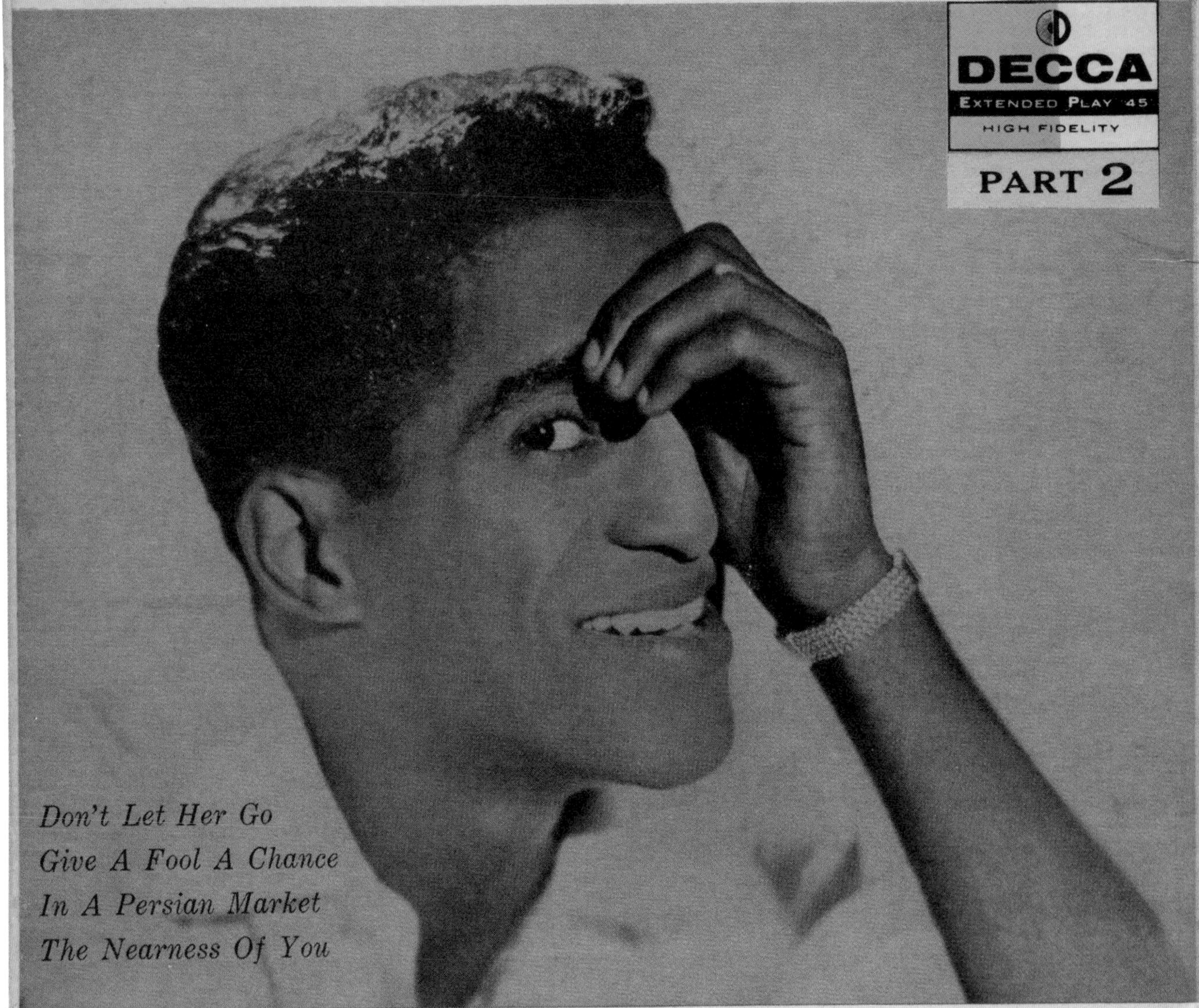

B-2518

BECAUSE OF YOU
COLD, COLD HEART
RAGS TO RICHES
STRANGER IN PARADISE

TONY BENNETT

COLUMBIA

HALL
OF
FAME
series

® "Columbia" ® Marcas Reg. Printed in U. S. A.

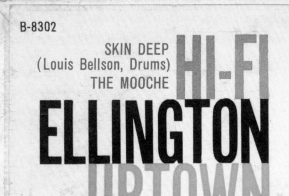

B-8302

SKIN DEEP
(Louis Bellson, Drums)
THE MOOCHE

HI-FI

ELLINGTON

UPTOWN

® "Columbia", "360", Marcas Reg. Printed in U. S. A.

COLUMBIA

EXTENDED PLAY

"360" SOUND

GUARANTEED
HIGH-FIDELITY

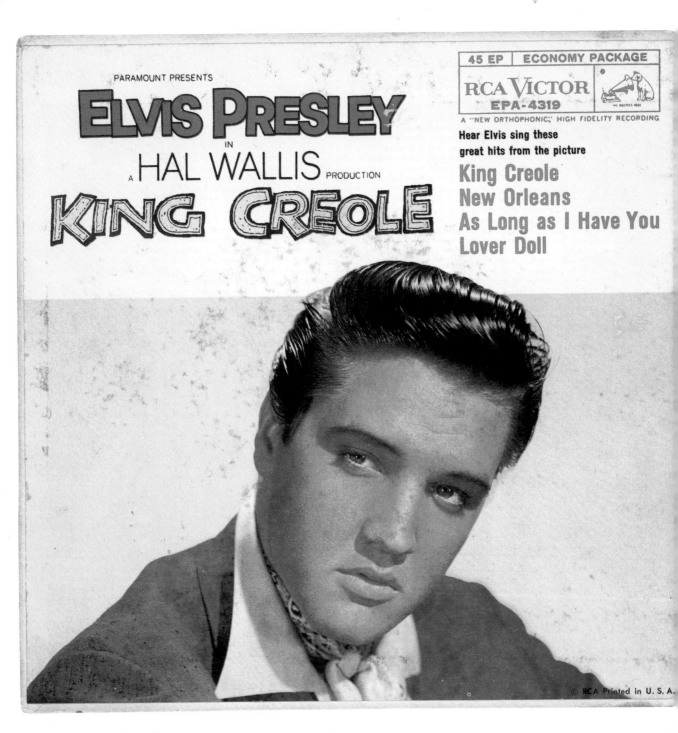

GOLD STANDARD SERIES

RCA VICTOR
45EP EPA-5141
A "NEW ORTHOPHONIC" HIGH FIDELITY RECORDING

VOLUME 3

A TOUCH OF GOLD ELVIS PRESLEY

Too Much
All Shook Up
Don't Ask
Me Why
Blue Moon of
Kentucky

© RCA Printed in U. S. A.

RCA VICTOR ®

45EP EPB-1134

A HIGH FIDELITY RECORDING

Dennis, Anyone?

MATT DENNIS

© RCA Printed in U.S.A.

DENNIS, ANYONE? ~ MATT DENNIS

EPB 1134

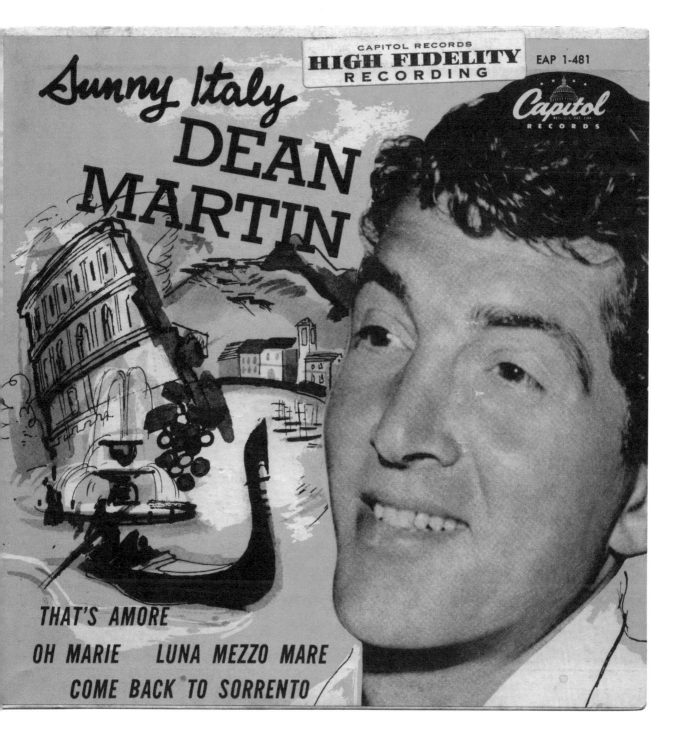

 **B-1562**

LIBERACE

by candlelight

TCHAIKOVSKY'S PIANO CONCERTO

I DON'T CARE

JALOUSIE

SEPTEMBER SONG

COLUMBIA *records*

m. g. monogram

Unforgettable

songs by
Nat 'King' Cole

CAPITOL RECORDS
HIGH FIDELITY
RECORDING

Capitol
RECORDS
REG. U.S. PAT. OFF.

PART **1** EAP 1-357

UNFORGETTABLE

PORTRAIT OF JENNIE

FOR SENTIMENTAL REASONS

RED SAILS IN THE SUNSET

Perfect for Dancing

RCA **VICTOR** ®
45EP EPB-1066
ENHANCED SOUND

WALTZES

Produced and prepared under the direction of the Fred Astaire Dance Studios

© RCA PRINTED IN U.S.A.

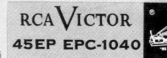

A "NEW ORTHOPHONIC" HIGH FIDELITY RECORDING

RCA VICTOR
45EP EPC-1040

BOBBY DUKOFF

his Tenor Sax and Orchestra

with the Ray Charles Chorus

SAX IN SILK

Do I Worry?
My Melancholy Baby
I Gotta Right to Sing the Blues
You Taught Me to Love Again
It's the Talk of the Town
In the Shade of the Old Apple Tree
I Can't Give You Anything but Love
Body and Soul
Let's Do It
Makin' Whoopee
You've Changed
Keep Cool

© RCA Printed in U.S.A.

B-2550

BE MY LIFE'S COMPANION
BLAME IT ON MY YOUTH
BLUES IN THE NIGHT
WHY FIGHT THE FEELING?

ROSEMARY CLOONEY

COLUMBIA

HALL OF FAME series

® "Columbia", ® Marcas Reg. Printed in U. S. A.

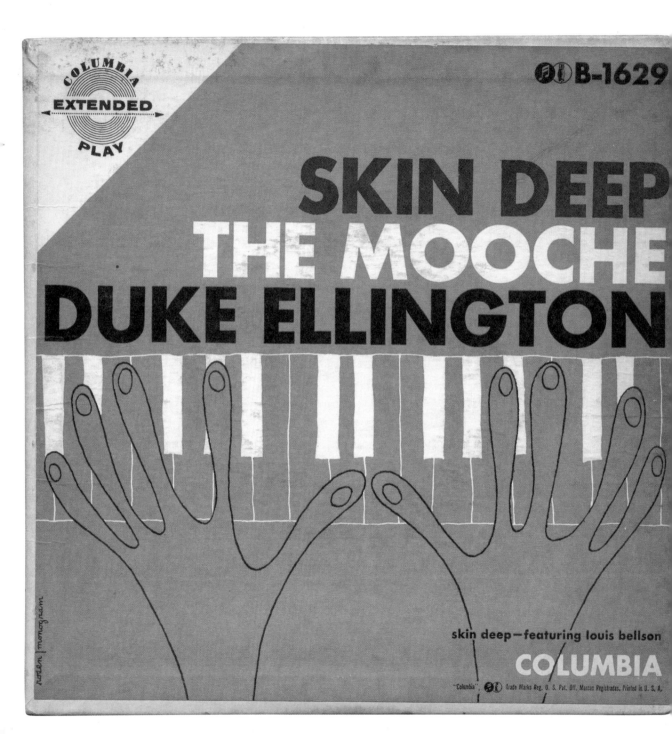

B-1524

SINGS
IRVING
BERLIN

FRANK Sinatra

ALWAYS
BLUE SKIES
HOW DEEP IS THE OCEAN
THEY SAY IT'S WONDERFUL

COLUMBIA RECORDS

COLUMBIA EXTENDED PLAY

graber | monogram

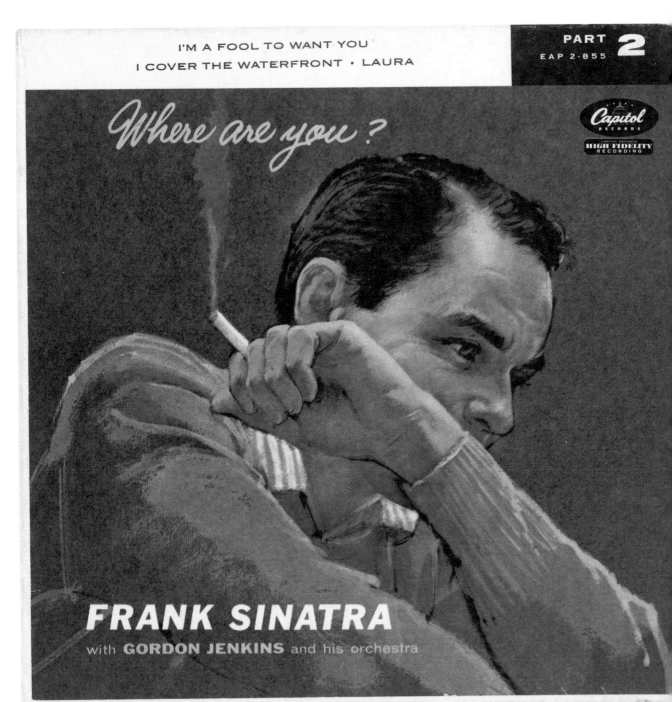

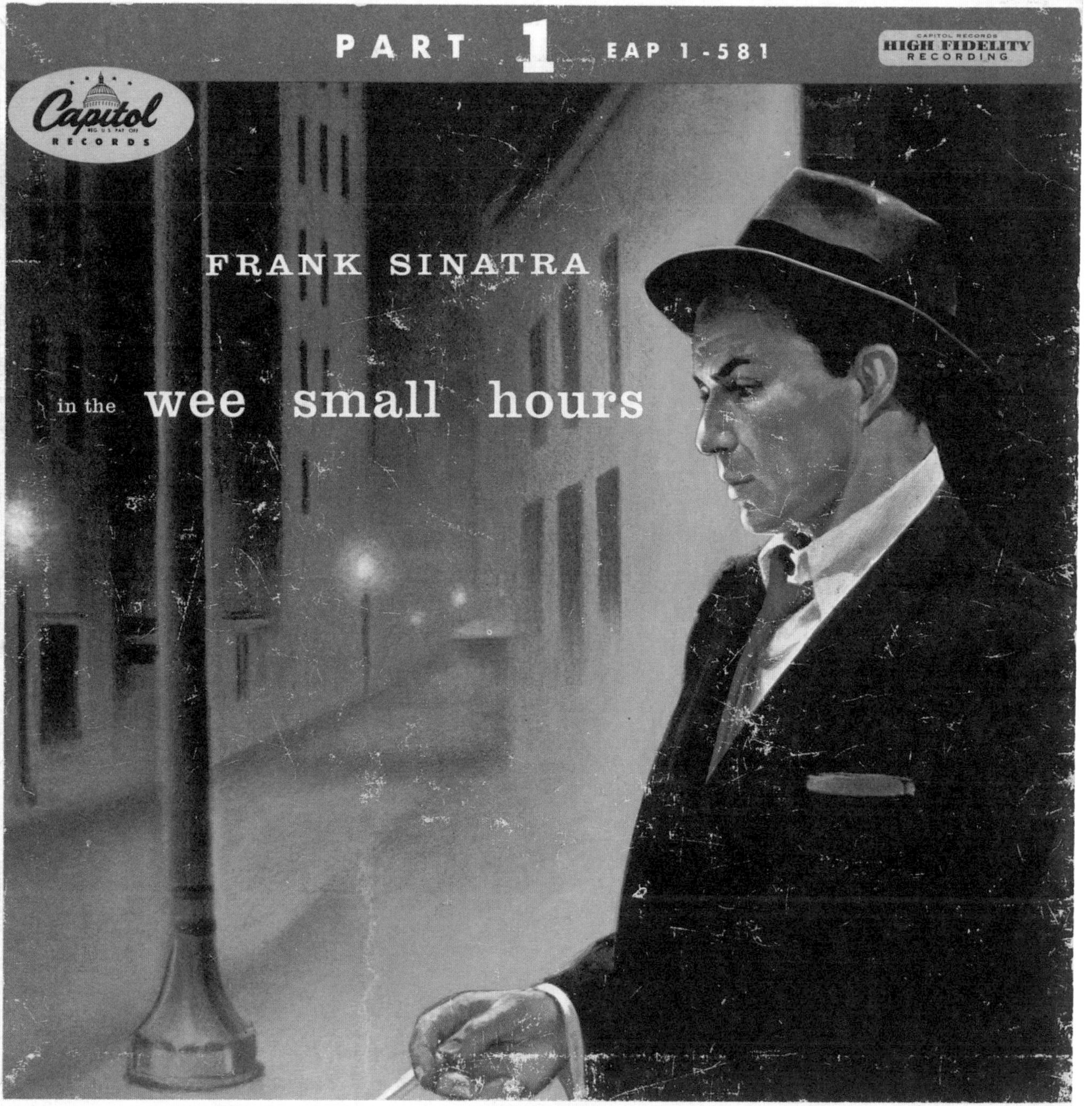
PART 1
EAP 1-581
CAPITOL RECORDS
HIGH FIDELITY
RECORDING
Capitol
RECORDS
FRANK SINATRA
in the wee small hours

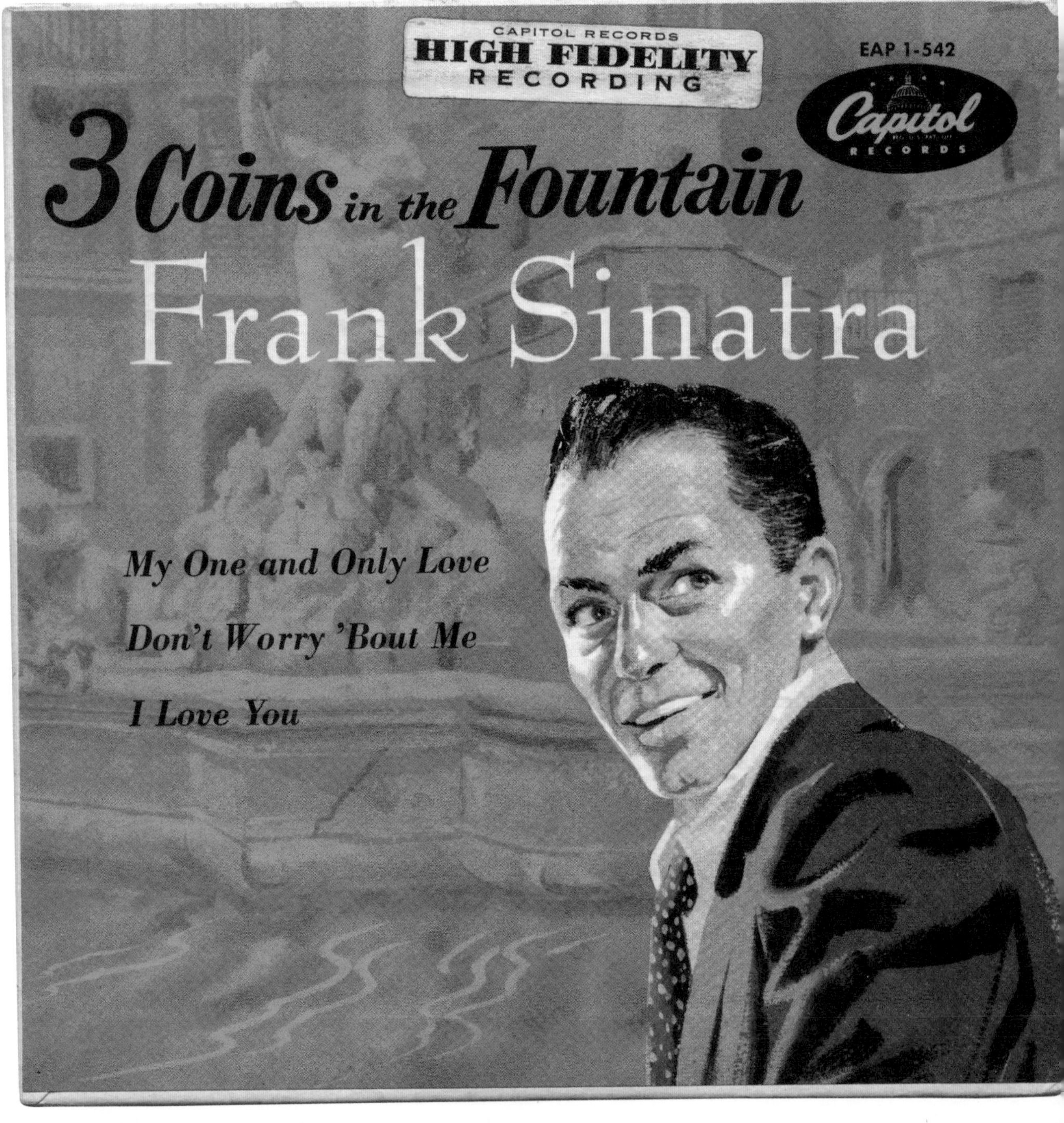

CAPITOL RECORDS
HIGH FIDELITY RECORDING

EAP 1-542

Capitol RECORDS

3 *Coins* in the *Fountain*

Frank Sinatra

My One and Only Love

Don't Worry 'Bout Me

I Love You

COLUMBIA
EXTENDED
PLAY

B-1702

SINATRA

FRANK
SINGS
JEROME
KERN

Ol' Man River

All The Things You Are

Why Was I Born?

The Song Is You

COLUMBIA

lubell | monogram

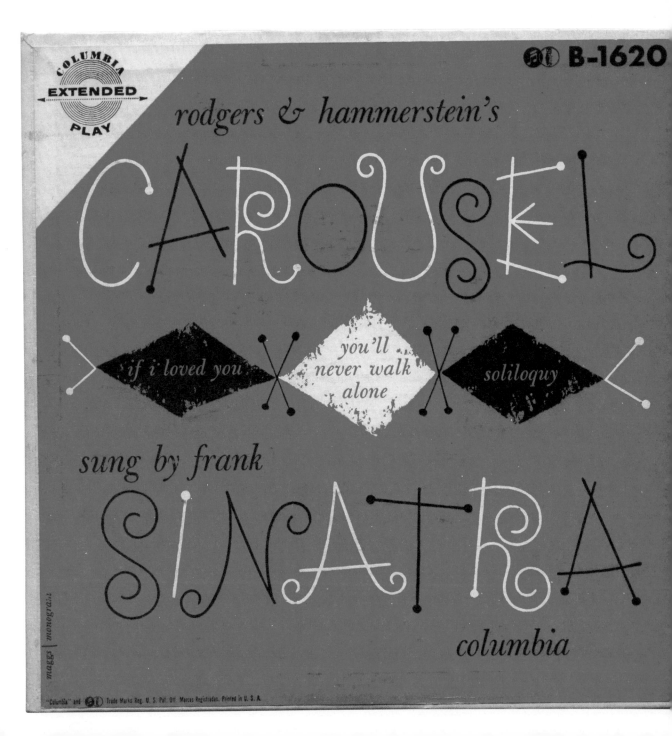

stan getz plays

tootsie roll
strike up the band
imagination
tor stompers only

BURT GOLDBLATT

roost records
"45" extended play
EP 306   volume 4

EP4-
CHET BAKER
QUARTET
easy to love
batter up
isn't it romantic
this time the dream's on me
J. BRANDT
PACIFIC JAZZ
Produced by RICHARD BOCK

Verve

A PANORAMIC TRUE
HIGH FIDELITY RECORD

EPV-C-1712

Ella   Louis

Isn't This A Lovely Day
Cheek To Cheek

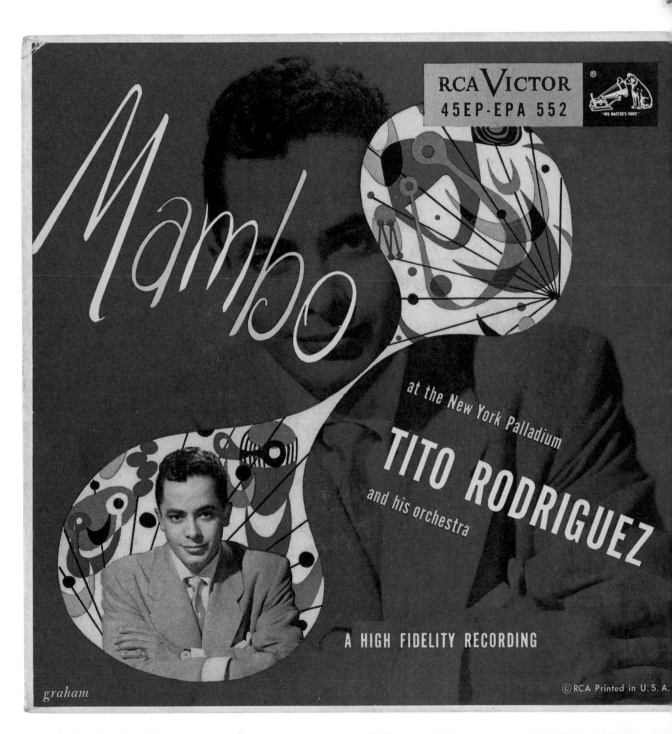

COLUMBIA EXTENDED PLAY

"Columbia" and ⓔⓒ Trade Marks Reg. U. S. Pat. Off. Marcas Registradas. Printed in U. S. A.

B-304

mambo at the waldorf

mambo at the waldorf
cuca
yo quiero un mambo
the peanut vendor
mambo o. k.
mondongo
mambo gallego
jamay

XAVIER CUGAT

columbia records

Jerry Lee Lewis

▶ Great Balls of Fire
and
▶ YOU WIN AGAIN

SUN 281

• A PRODUCT OF SUN RECORD CO. MEMPHIS TENN

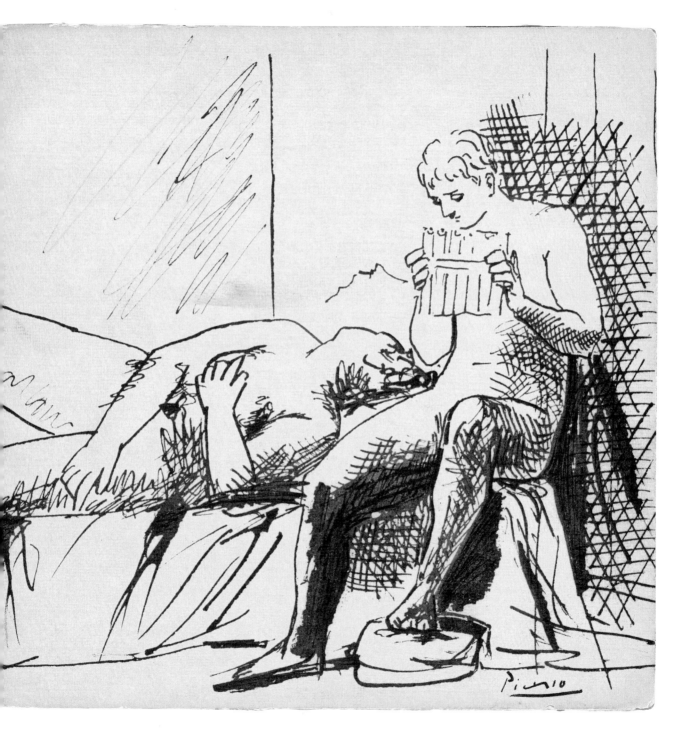

FROM MODS TO ROCKERS

SPENCER DRATE

19
60

A quick taste of pop music in the sixties: the British Invasion, the L.A. Sound, the San Francisco Sound, folk, hard rock, surf, Motown, hit-makers, teen idols, fan magazines, jukeboxes, psychedelics, Woodstock, the Fender Stratocaster, hippies, mods and rockers, the Twist. Through it all, there was the little 45— 7 inches of colorfully packaged black vinyl that defined an era.

The sleeves from the early 1960s share the sensibility of all those fan photos and magazines teens so eagerly devoured. Clean-cut smiling faces shot in colorful close-up distinguish covers for singles by the likes of Elvis Presley, Chubby Checker, Ricky Nelson, Paul Anka, and Bobby Rydell. With the British Invasion, pop sleeves, like pop music, gradually adopted a more provocative stance, and designers found themselves interpreting music visually. The Beatles' singles progress from the "mod" look—with signature bowl haircuts—of *She Loves You* (photograph by Dezo Hoffman) to the psychedelic *I Am A Walrus*—a shift that reflected the change in their musical style. The Rolling Stones started out as hipsters on their classic *Five by Five* cover, which had no identifying type, just a photo of the group posed as a threatening, if somewhat arty, gang. They went "rocker" for the cover of *As Tears Go By,* and for *She's A Rainbow* paid homage to the Beatles' *Sgt. Pepper's* album.

With the new emphasis on photography, type design became something of a lost art, though a few covers, such as Tom Jones's *She's A Lady,* carried on the typographic traditions of the 1950s. Back covers were often egregiously ugly informational treatments in black type. One notable exception was Simon & Garfunkel's double-headed sleeve for *The Boxer*, which had front/back photos of the two singers.

The arrival of the psychedelic movement in the late 1960s propelled illustration and typographic virtuosity back into style. The influential work of artists such as Peter Max, Victor Moscoso, Rick Griffin, Kelley and Mouse, and R. Crumb conveyed a sense of freedom that resonated with musicians, designers, and the public, and their styles were carried over into the design of singles covers. Blue Cheer's *Summertime Blues* is a classic of this genre.

The 1960s were extraordinary years for the design of 45s, and the era's two greatest bands, the Beatles and the Stones, were its design bellwethers.

SPENCER DRATE is an author and designer for the music industry whose clients have included the Beach Boys, Bon Jovi, and U2. He is the author of *Designing for Music* and *Cool Type*, and is a member of the Grammy Award committee for record design.

RCA VICTOR
47-7810
A "NEW ORTHOPHONIC" HIGH FIDELITY RECORDING

ELVIS PRESLEY

Are you lonesome to-night?

I gotta know

© RCA Printed in U.S.A.

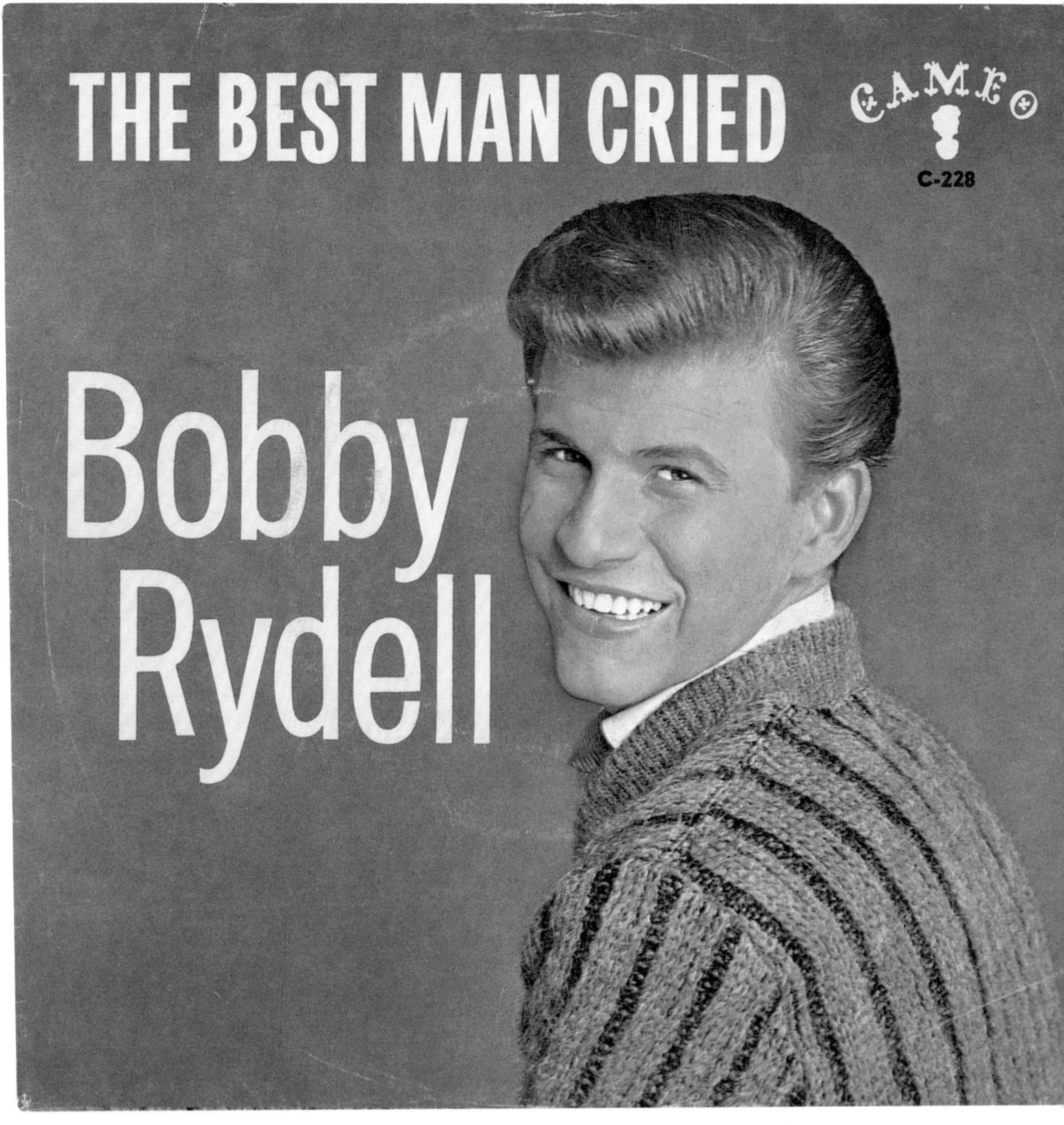
THE BEST MAN CRIED
CAMEO
C-228
Bobby
Rydell

ABOUT THIS THING CALLED LOVE ·
STRING ALONG

45 RPM
Chancellor

C-1047

FABIAN

FABIAN is currently appearing in
Jerry Wald's
20th Century-Fox Film "Hound Dog Man".

Soon to be seen in
20th Century-Fox's "High Time"
starring Bing Crosby.

FABIAN INTERNATIONAL FAN CLUB
BOX 234 — DEPT. F
PLANETARIUM STATION
NEW YORK 24, N. Y.
DIST. BY AM-PAR RECORD CORP.

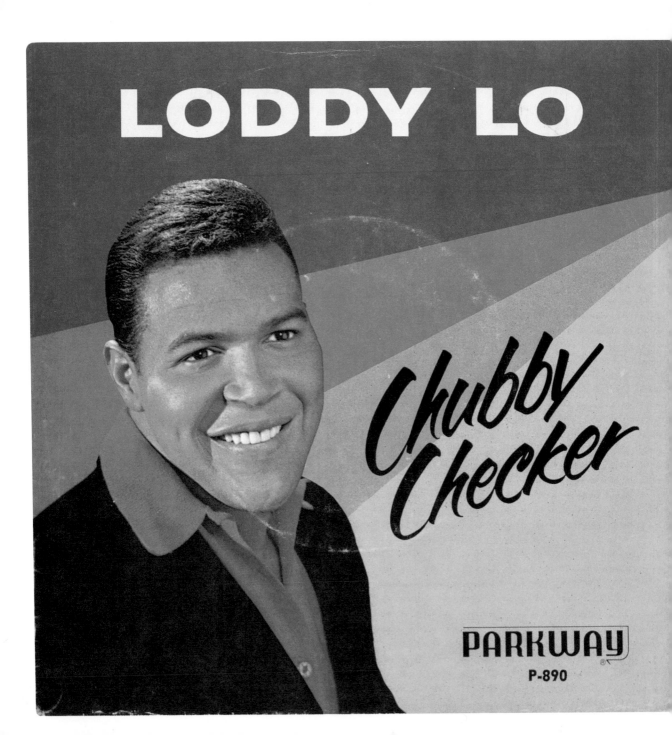

K-13386

ROY ORBISON
RIDE AWAY b/w WONDERING

MGM
HIGH FIDELITY

®© Metro-Goldwyn-Mayer, Inc./Printed in U.S.A.

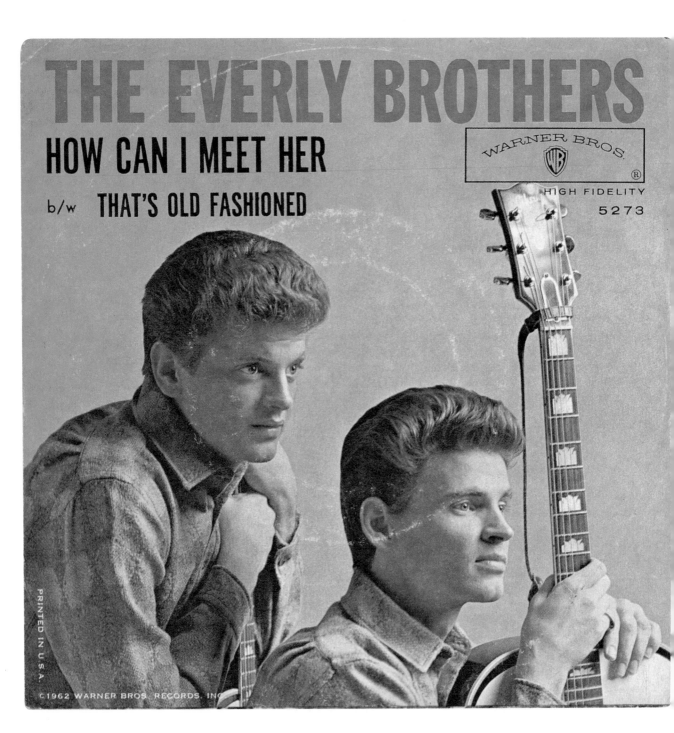

TONIGHT - MY LOVE - TONIGHT

I'M JUST A FOOL ANYWAY

ABC-PARAMOUNT
FULL COLOR FIDELITY ®
10194

PAUL ANKA

PAUL ANKA FAN CLUB
NATIONAL HEADQUARTERS
SHYANNA
P.O. Box 466, Times Sq. Station
New York 36, N. Y.

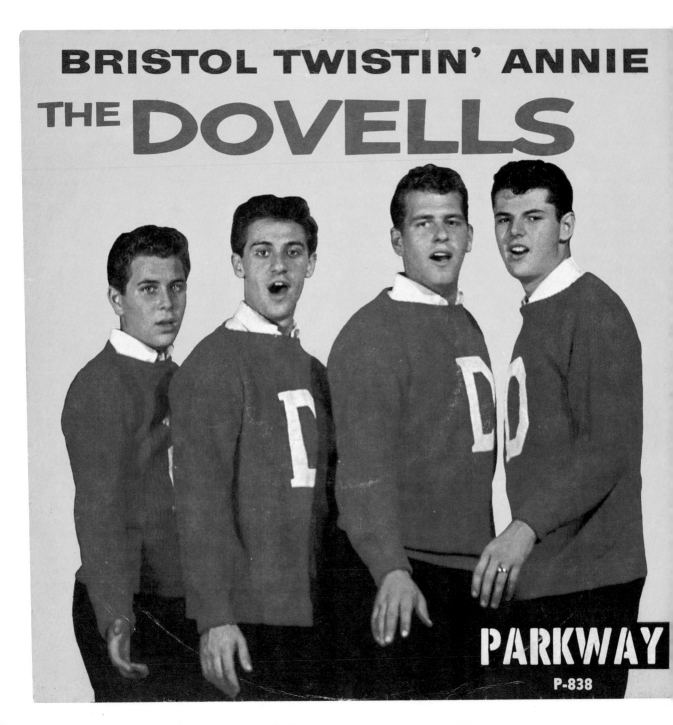

BRISTOL TWISTIN' ANNIE

THE DOVELLS

PARKWAY

P-838

THE BEATLES
"SHE LOVES YOU"

SWAN
S-4152

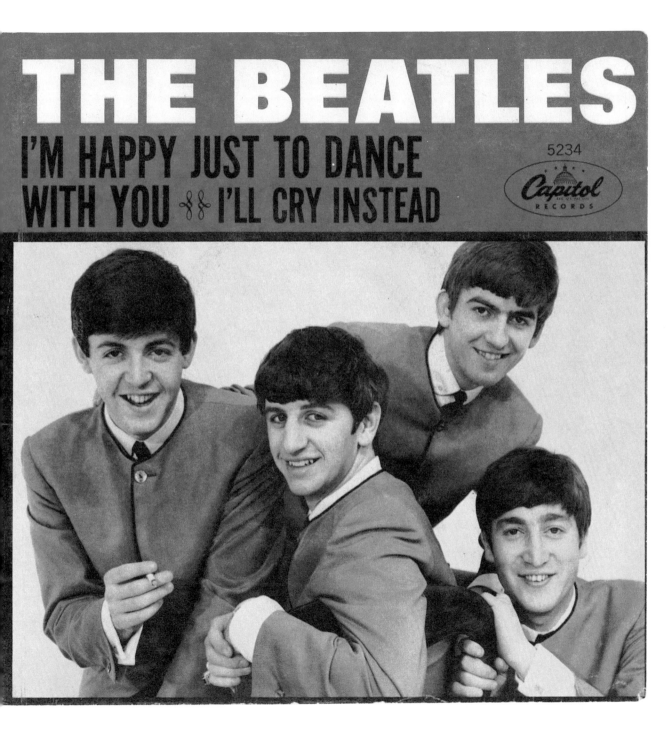

LOVE ME DO

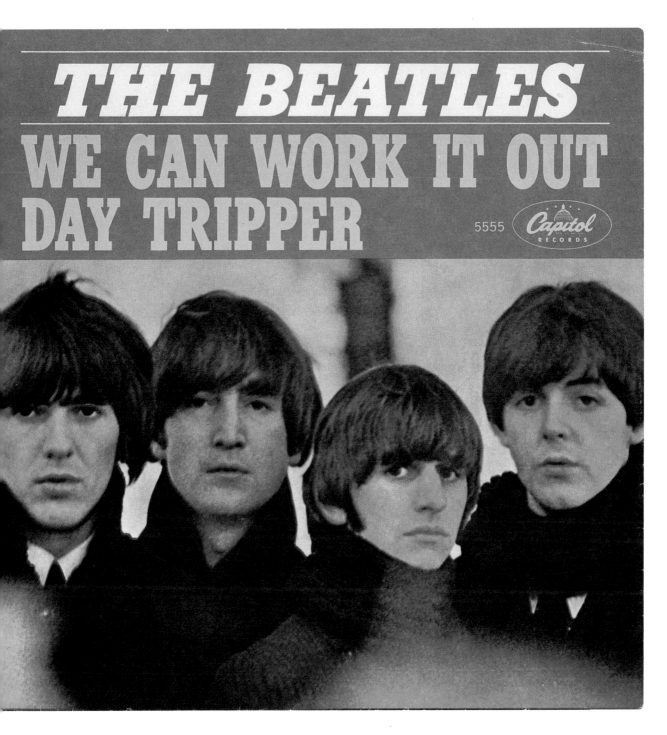

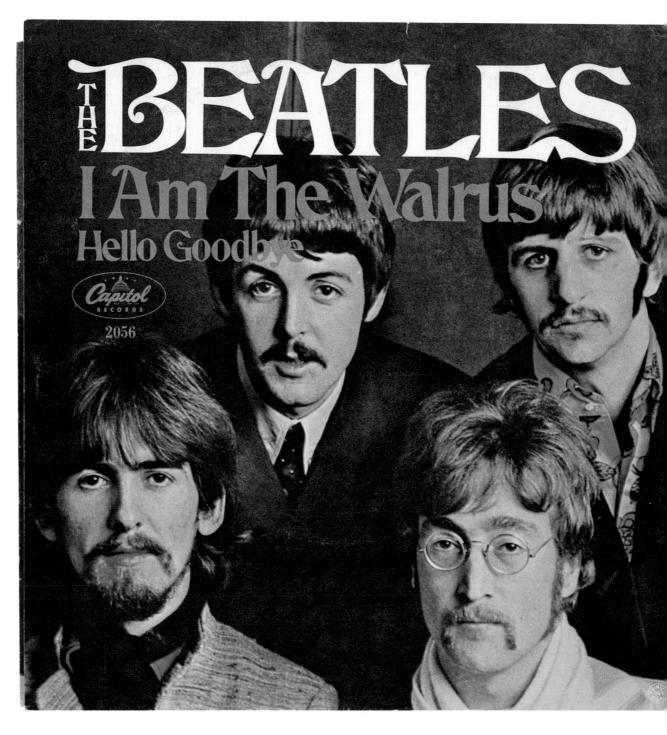

mono DFE 8590

DECCA

as tears go by
THE ROLLING STONES*

45-9808

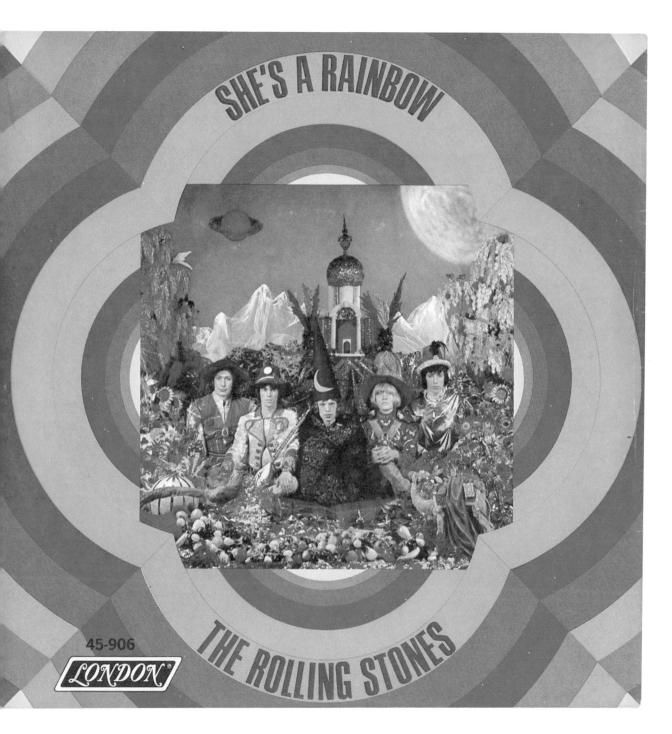

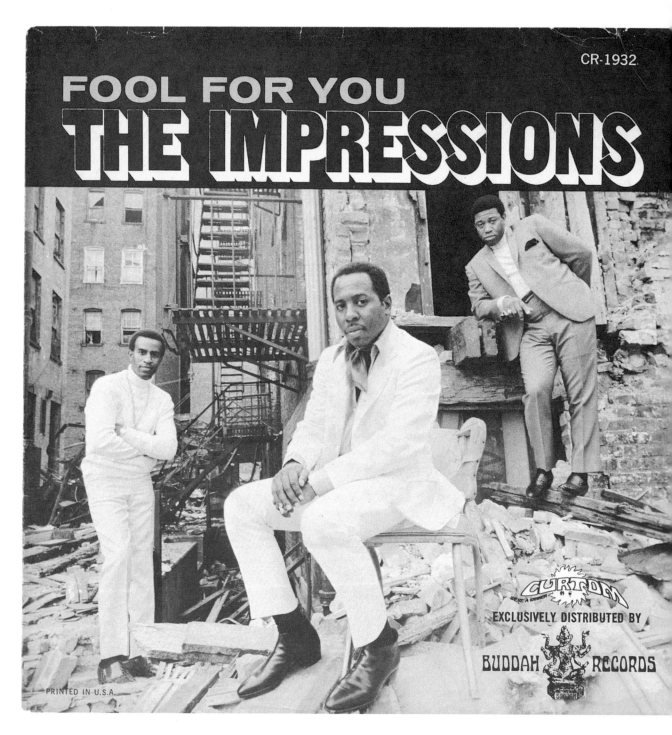

MY GIRL
"TALKING, BOUT" NOBODY BUT MY BABY

THE TEMPTATIONS

GORDY-7038

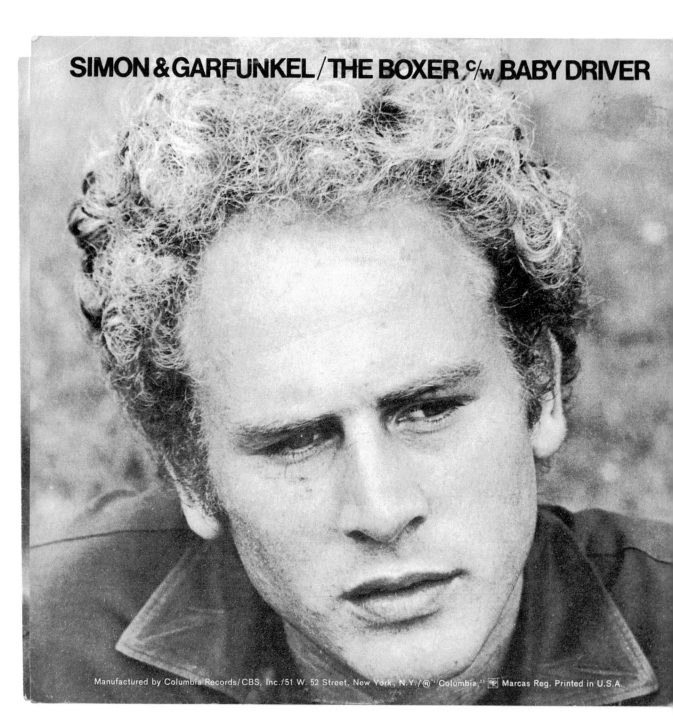

SIMON & GARFUNKEL / THE BOXER c/w BABY DRIVER

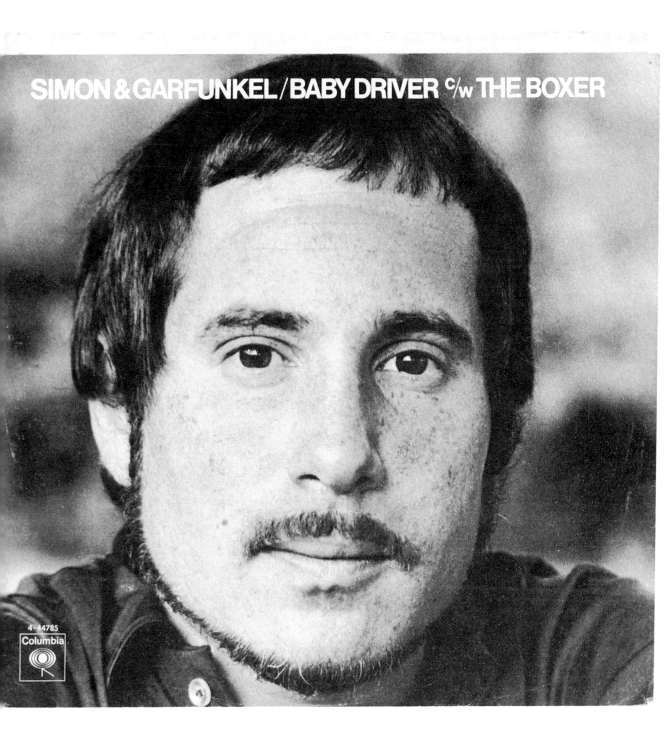

VRS·35061

"Who Am I"

Country Joe and The Fish

VANGUARD
RECORDS

DESIGN/JULES HALFANT

PHOTO/JOEL BRODSKY

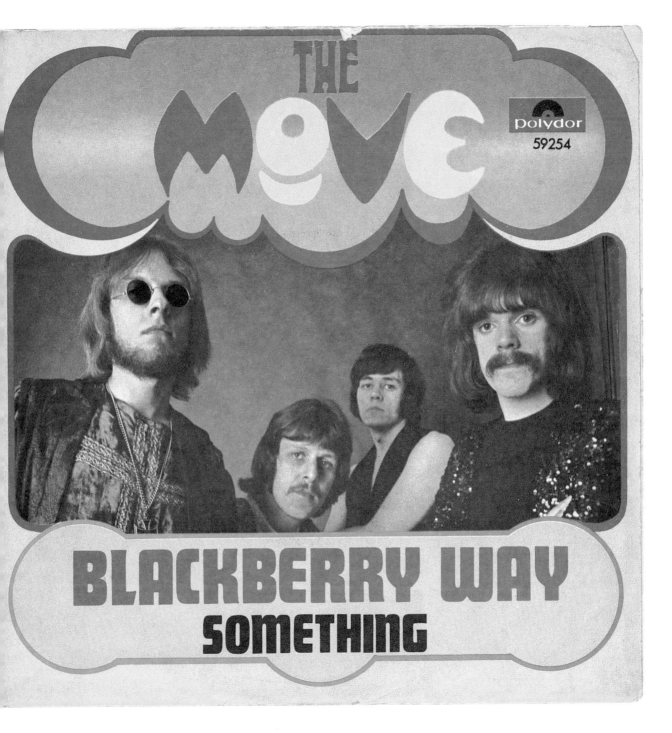

AS 2165

MANFRED MANN
SHA LA LA

B/W JOHN HARDY

ASCOT

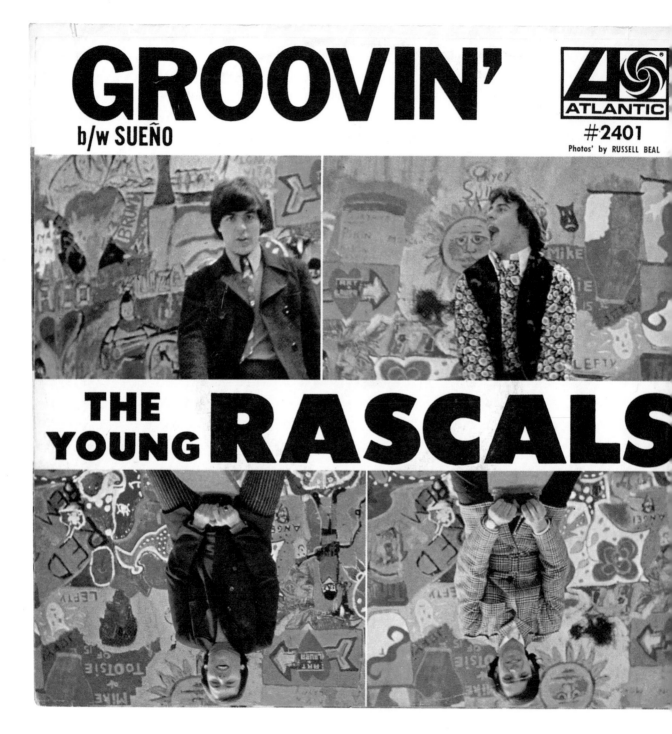

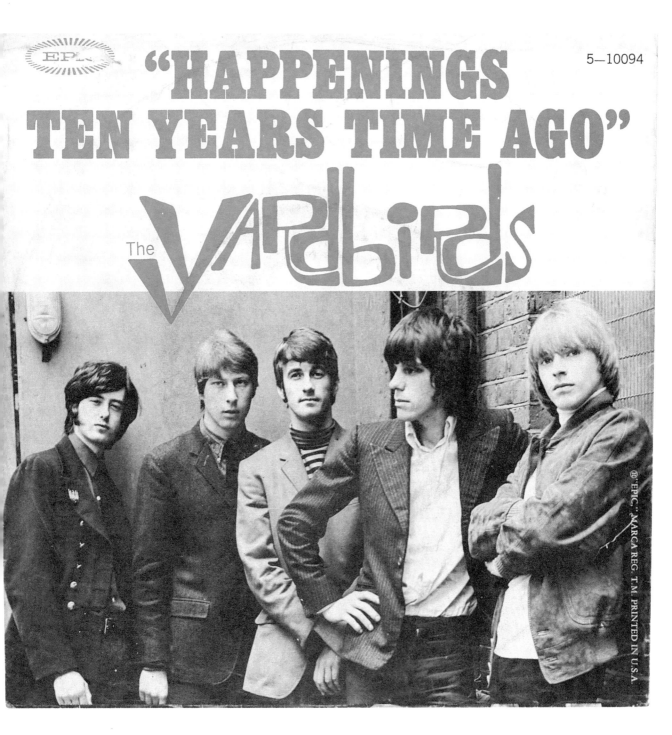

DONOVAN

SUNSHINE SUPERMAN

EPIC

5-10045

®"EPIC". Marca Reg. T.M. PRINTED IN U.S.A.

Simon and Garfunkel at the Zoo

COLUMBIA

4-44046

chas b blackman

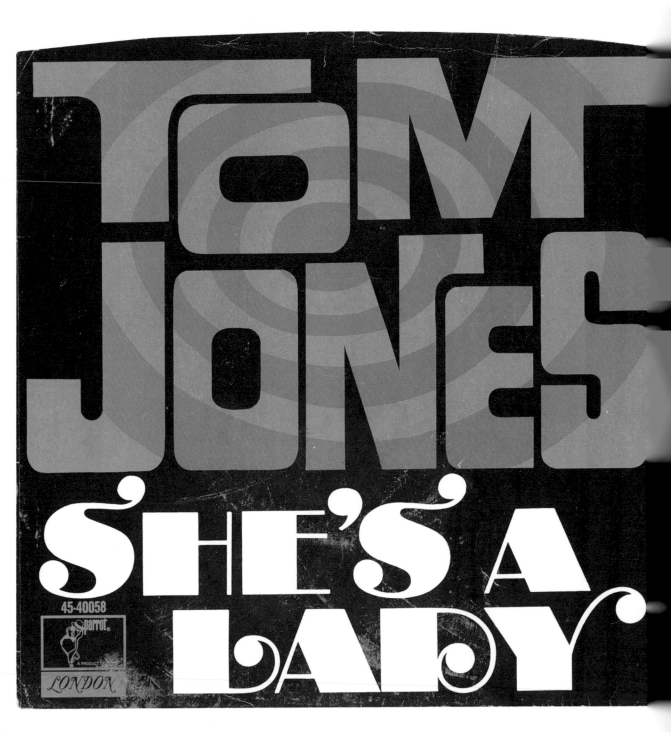

KINKY BOOTS

PATRICK MACNEE & HONOR BLACKMAN

19 70

ROCK AND ROLL RELICS

ROGER DEAN

For those of us who came of age when rock and roll was still in its infancy, 45s were holy relics. It's impossible to overestimate the allure of these little black discs. We listened to them and then used them to decorate our bedrooms. Rock changed the world, and singles were the vehicle of that change.

Growing up in England and Hong Kong during the late fifties, the LP represented riches beyond my comprehension—I never actually knew anyone who owned one until I was well into my teenage years. Accessible grandeur was represented by the EP, with its printed color cover. My first purchase, a major investment, was the Elvis Presley EP *Good Rockin' Tonight,* which I followed with singles from Ricky Nelson, the Everly Brothers, and Buddy Holly—the amazing "Peggy Sue." The idea that I could actually make covers like these myself was irresistible.

I designed my first album cover, for the band Gun, at the end of 1968. The band's management approved a Boschian painting of hell (produced before I even knew of Hieronymus Bosch), because it went with the album's lead track, "Race with the Devil." That started my career. But by then the single was pretty much relegated to pop, and no one really knew whether it was intended for singles charts in its own right or to promote LPs. In an age of rock operas and "concept" albums, many bands rejected the very idea of the single—and the singles charts—in the first place. Others simply lacked interest.

In a perfect world, the designs for single covers would have been the wild and wooly spin-offs or discarded ideas developed while creating the larger LP covers. The single was the natural venue for these experiments, a medium in which a designer could try things out, relax a bit, have fun. Sometimes this was just what happened. But usually not. With so many disinterested bands, indecisive record labels, miniscule budgets, and conservative marketing departments, singles were too often frustrating exercises in disappointment rather than crucibles of artistic creativity.

Looking back, it's amazing just how much great stuff actually got made. A lot of it came from the group of artists operating out of San Francisco, whose work is too often lumped together. I bought the Grateful Dead album *Aoxomoxoa* a year before I could afford a record player simply for Rick Griffin's cover. Rick did tragically few pieces, and only a few singles, but what he did do was wonderful. His work, and that of so many unheralded designers, remains an inspiration.

ROGER DEAN is an artist and designer whose fantasy dreamscapes have graced album covers for bands including Yes, Asia, Pink Floyd, and many others. He lives outside of Brighton, England.

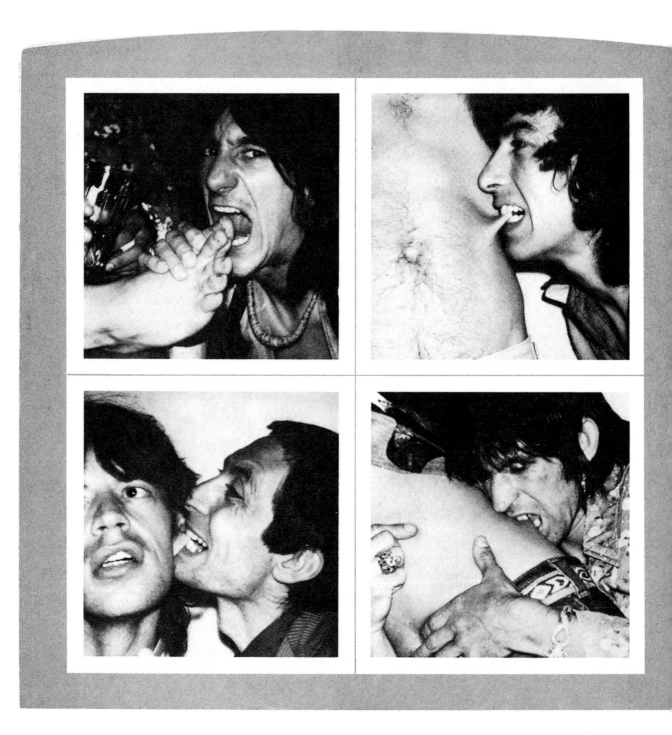

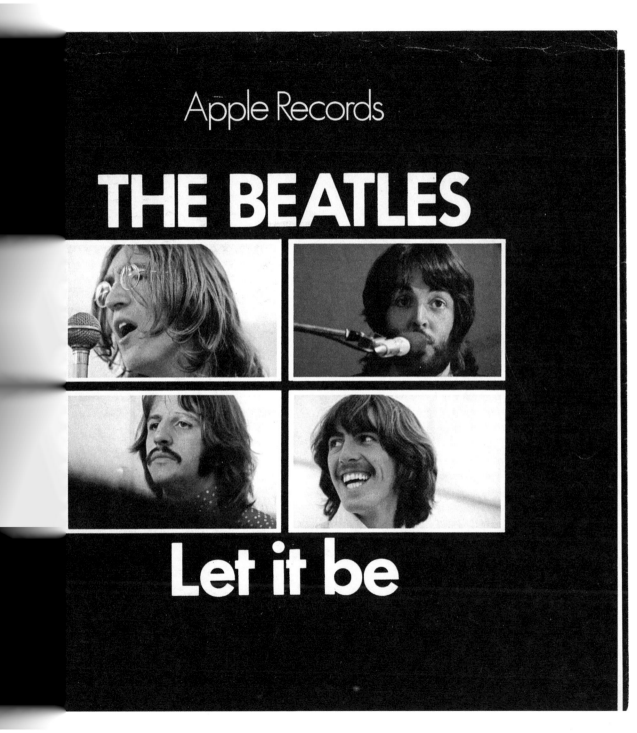

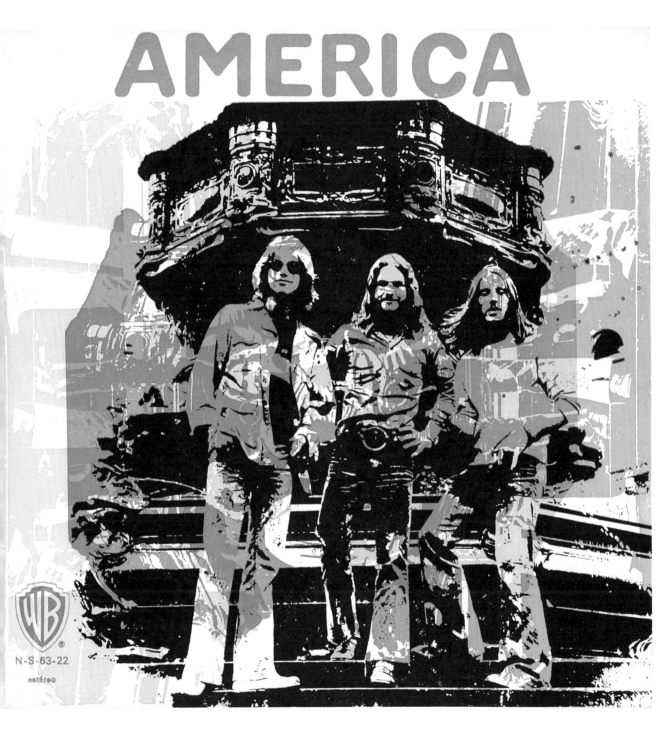

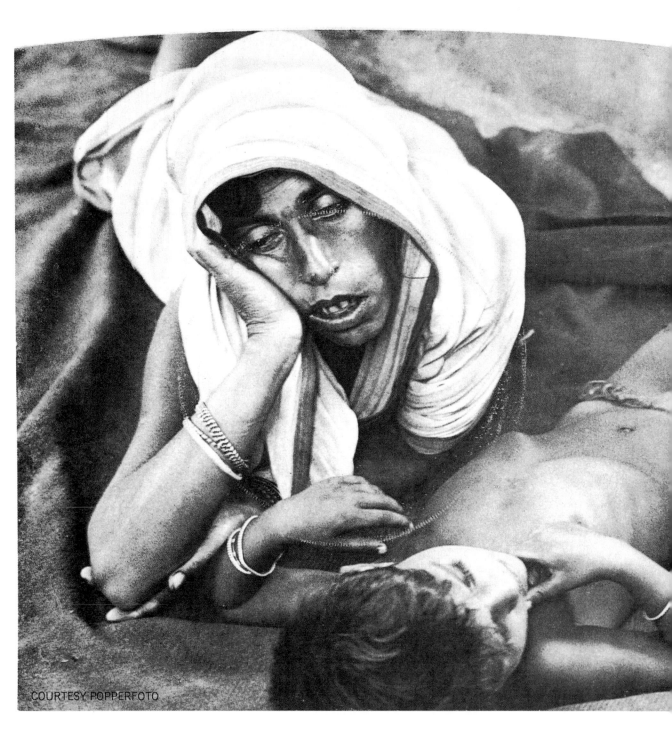

CAT STEVENS
Oh Very Young

AM-1503

THE FOUNDATIONS

BUILD ME UP BUTTERCUP

BABY NOW THAT I'VE FOUND YOU

10.525-A

PYE RECORDS

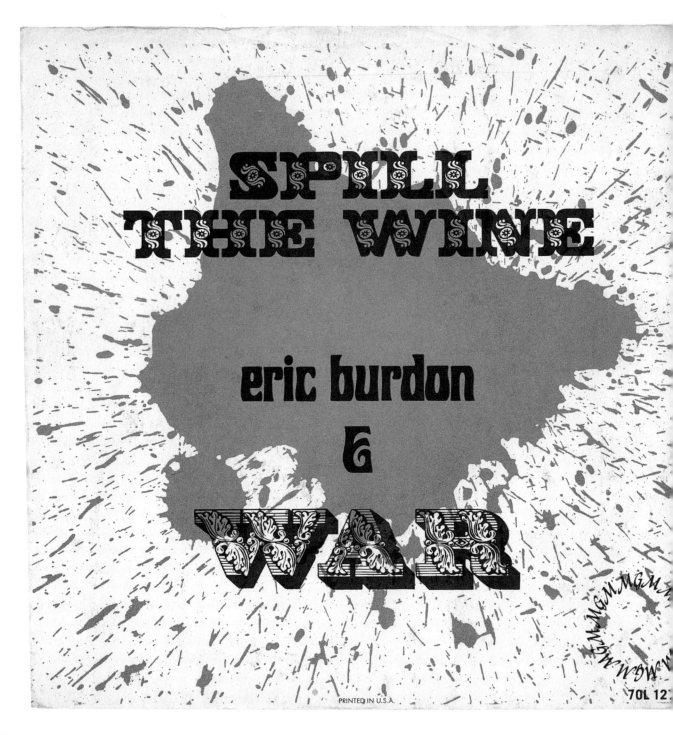

SPILL THE WINE

eric burdon & WAR

PRINTED IN U.S.A.

70L 12?

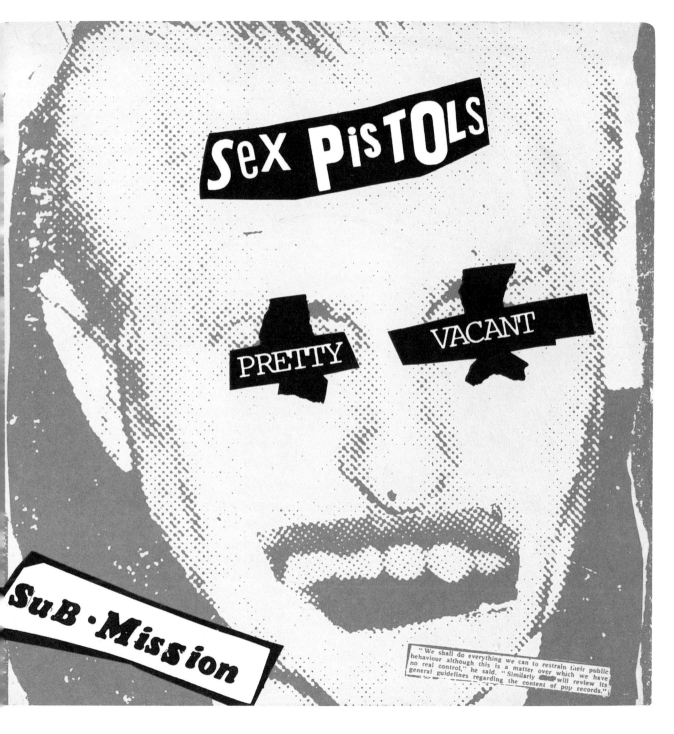

PUBLIC Image LTD

TURSDAY SEPTEMBER 31 1978

VIRGIN VS 228

The girls who drove me to tea, by Donut's wife Carol

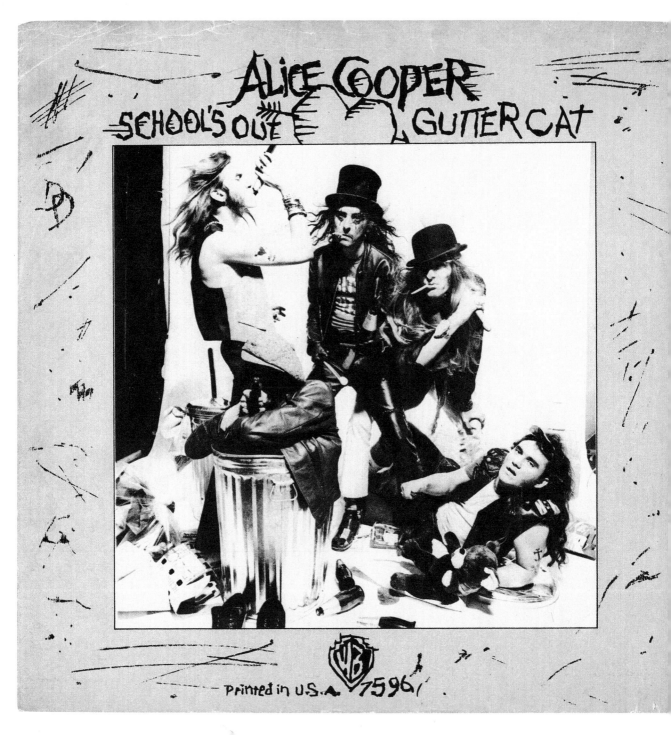

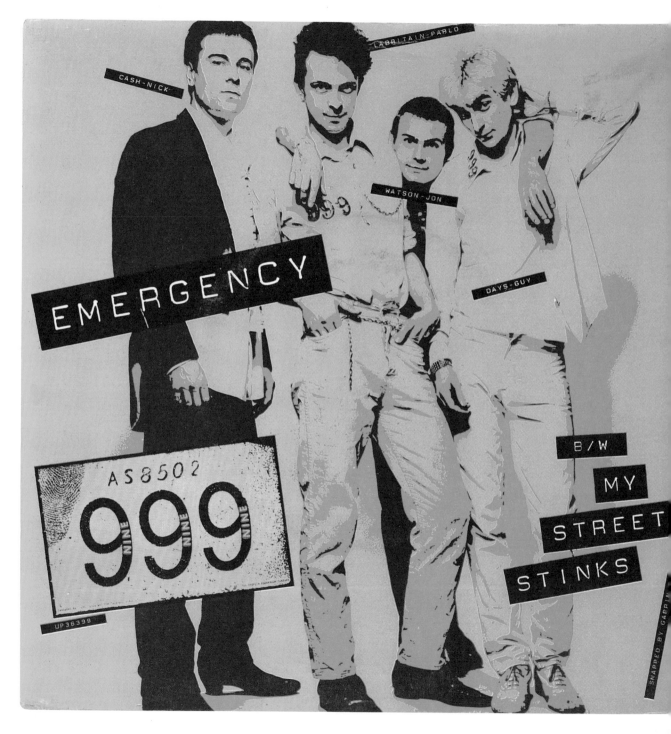

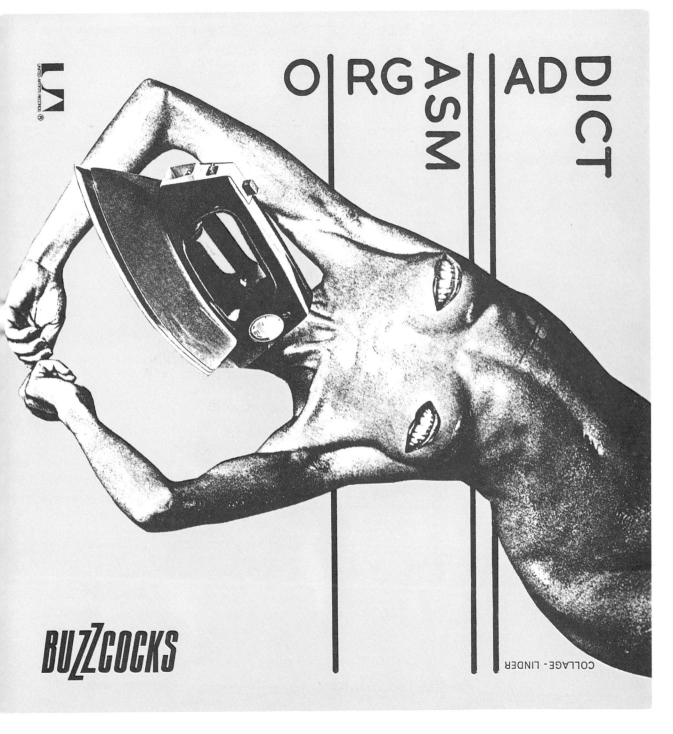

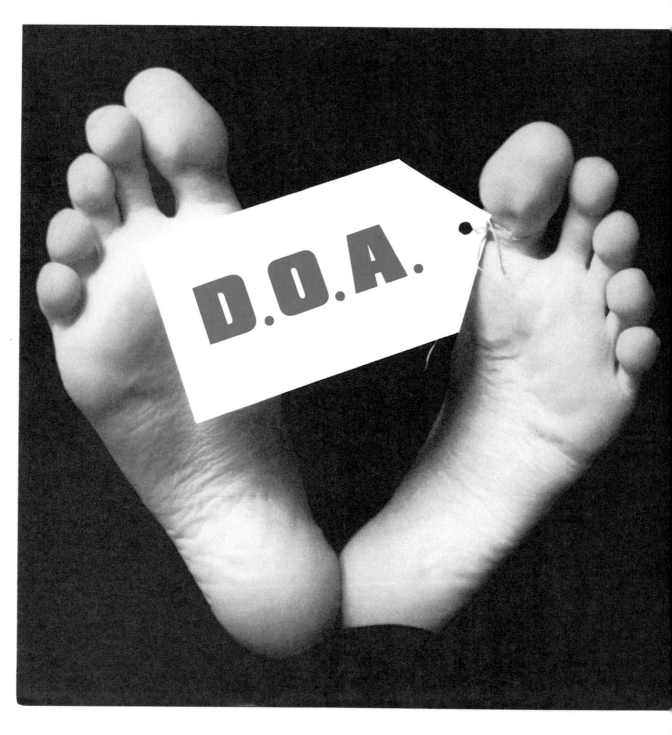

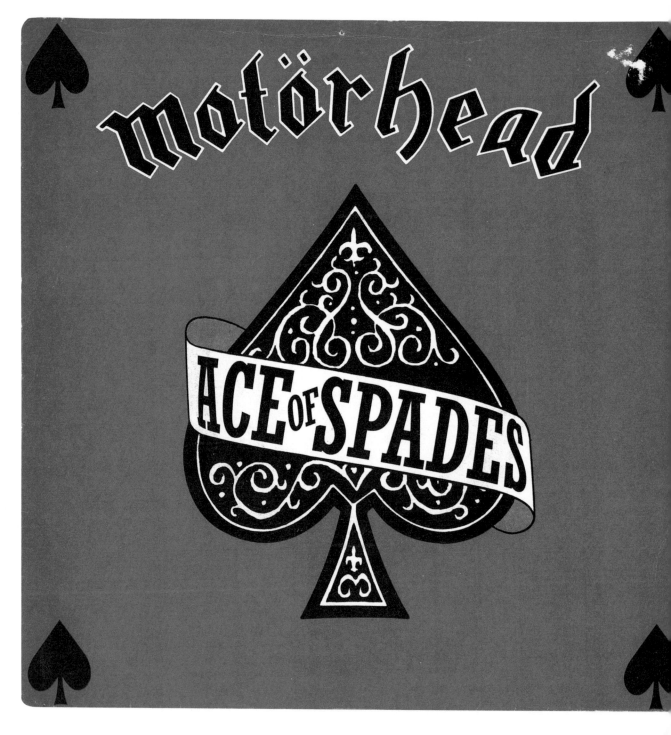

TALKING HEADS

FULL GOSPEL
TABERNACLE
PASTOR · AL GREEN

TAKE ME TO THE RIVER

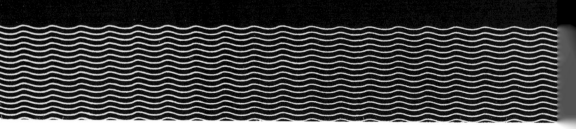

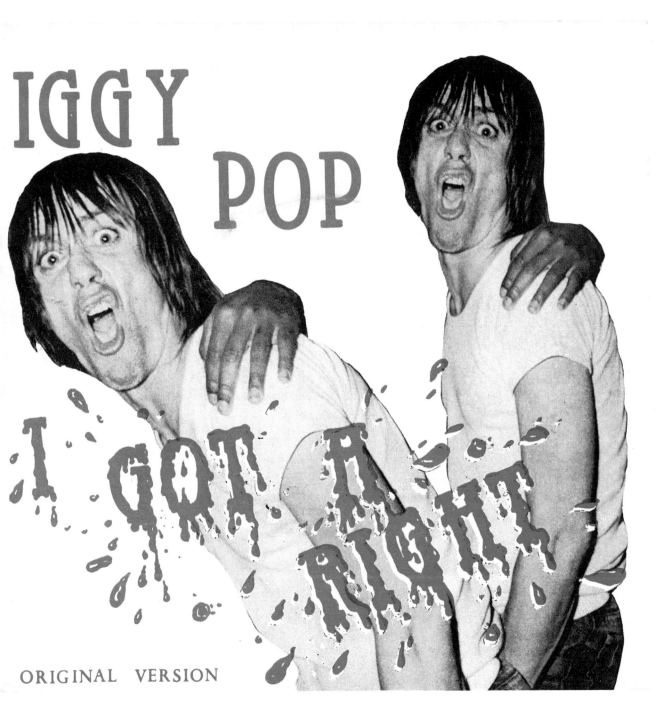

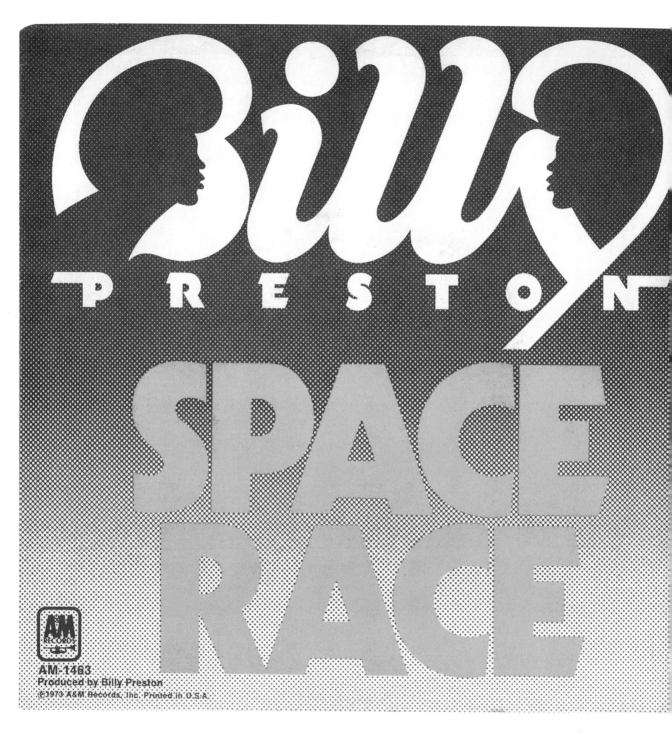

CR 1978

CURTIS MAYFIELD

Super Fly

GRAND FUNK

Shinin'On

Photo: Lynn Goldsmith

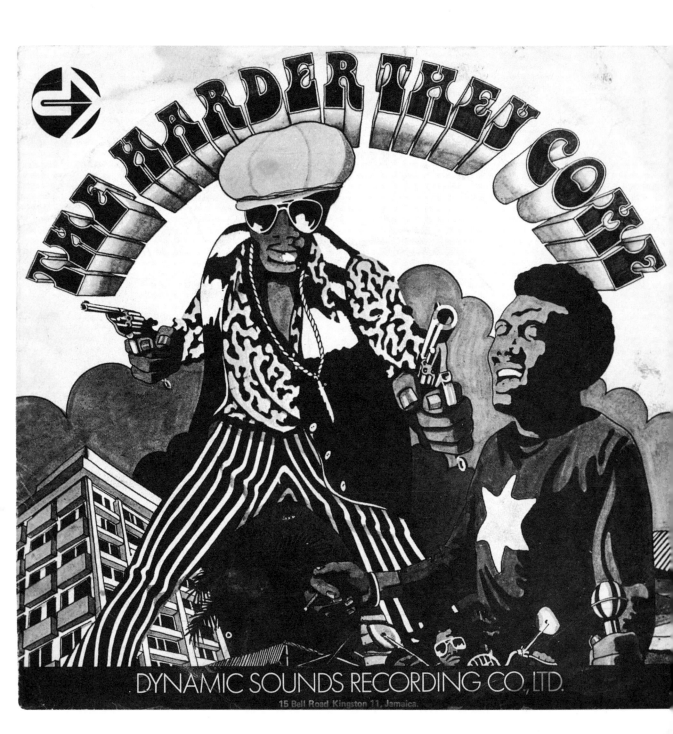

HIGH AND LOW

BOB GROSSWEINER

The 7-inch sleeves from the 1980s exhibited a startling range of sensibility, from the warmth of John Lennon and Yoko Ono smooching in close-up on the cover of Lennon's *(Just Like) Starting Over* to the intergalactic spaceships of Boston's *We're Ready*. There was high art (The Rolling Stones' *One Hit (To The Body)*, with its Francesco Clemente reproduction), kitch (The B-52's' *Rock*), simple but effective graphic design (Attention's *Zero Hour/Chapel of Love*), and a great deal of commercial pulp (Aretha Franklin in a pink Cadillac riding down the *Freeway of Love*).

As ever, the best covers were graphic distillations of the music they advertised. With the rise of synthetic sounds and New Wave came a stylized sensibility as seen in the playful designs for Depeche Mode's *Get the Balance Right!* and Supertramp's *Cannonball*. As the decade progressed, this simple visual language evolved into a more dramatic style, with bold type and eye-catching graphics, as with Visions' *It's a Choice*, U-Men's *Solid Action*, and Blurt's *A Fish Needs a Bike*. Sleeves from smaller, independent labels outside the music industry's New York–Los Angeles nexus were generally the most experimental. Thug's *Dad/Thug* (from Australia's Black Eye label) is a punky collage of doodles. Neef's *23*, from designer Bruce Licher and his Independent Project Press, has an extremely thick cardboard sleeve and letterpress type.

In an era of corporate power, logos and signature branding styles became ever more important. Kiss had their gothic type, the Stones an omnipresent tongue (adulterated to chilling effect for *She's So Cold*). Singles generally imitated the cover designs of the LPs from which they were drawn—that Lennon-Ono kiss came right from their *Double Fantasy* album. Some references were slightly more oblique: Supertramp's *Cannonball* design is an extension of the evolutionary man concept from the back of their LP *Brother Where You Bound?* Many of the sleeves had the same art work on both sides to ensure record stores did not promote the B-side when the single was put on a sales rack.

Shock was a standard design tool. Def Leppard's *Animal* and The Cure's *Wild Flower* do it with Goth type and illustration; Pat Benatar's *Invincible* and Deborah Harry's Andy Warhol–designed *French Kiss* use amped-up, in-your-face photography for attention-grabbing effect. But the most powerful cover from this decade, at least in retrospect, is surely Lennon's *Watching the Wheels*. Here we see John and Yoko walking nonchalantly out of the Dakota, their New York apartment house, John looking casually out at the camera just a few feet from where he would be fatally shot by a deranged fan on 8 October 1980.

BOB GROSSWEINER is an award-winning journalist who has been writing about rock and roll since 1973. His music criticism has appeared in some two hundred publications.

John Lennon

(Just Like)
Starting Over

Produced by John Lennon, Yoko Ono and Jack Douglas

John Lennon
Watching The Wheels

Joan Jett and the Blackhearts
Fake Friends

MCA-52240

BRYAN ADAMS

straight from the heart

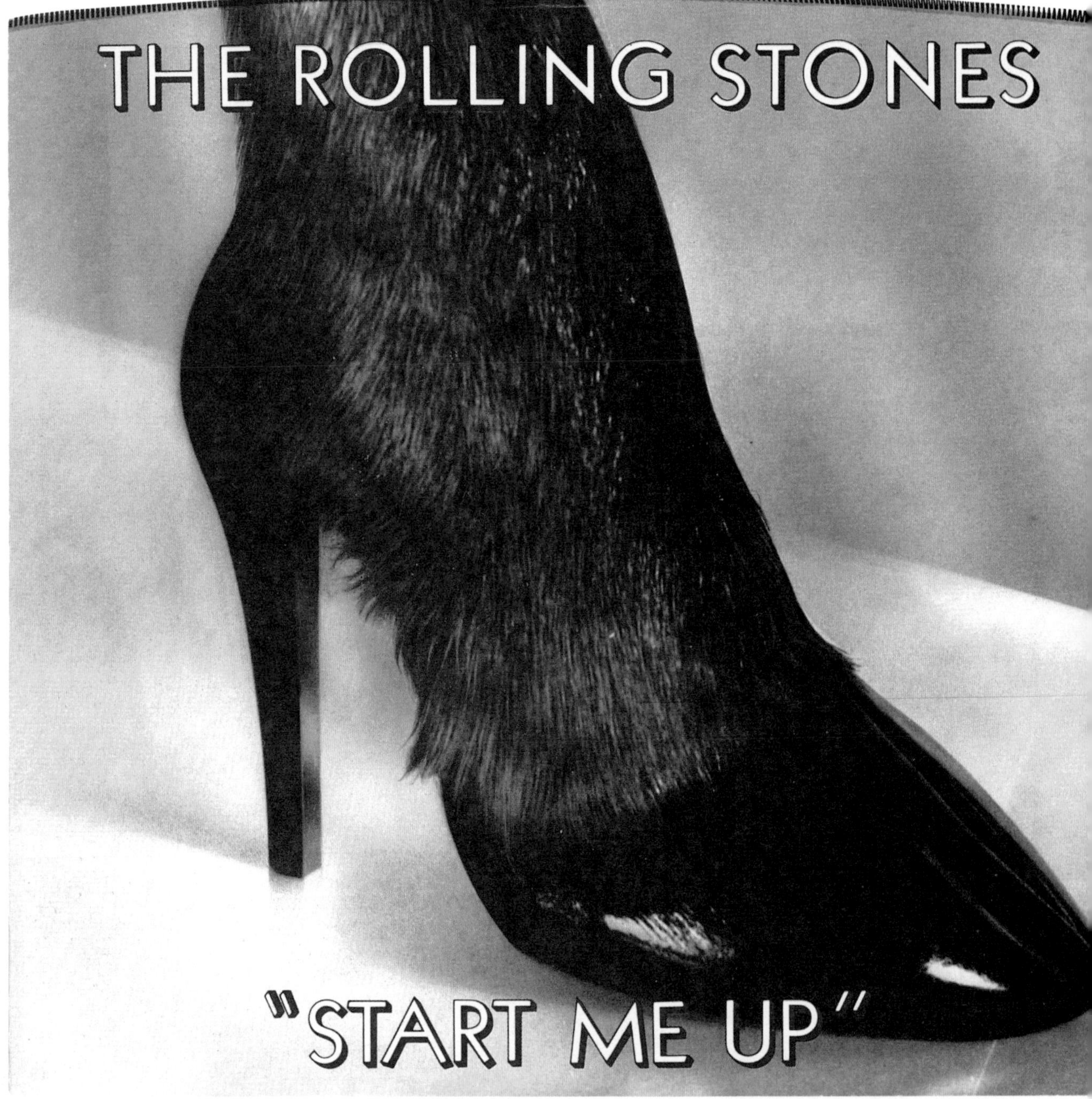
THE ROLLING STONES
"START ME UP"

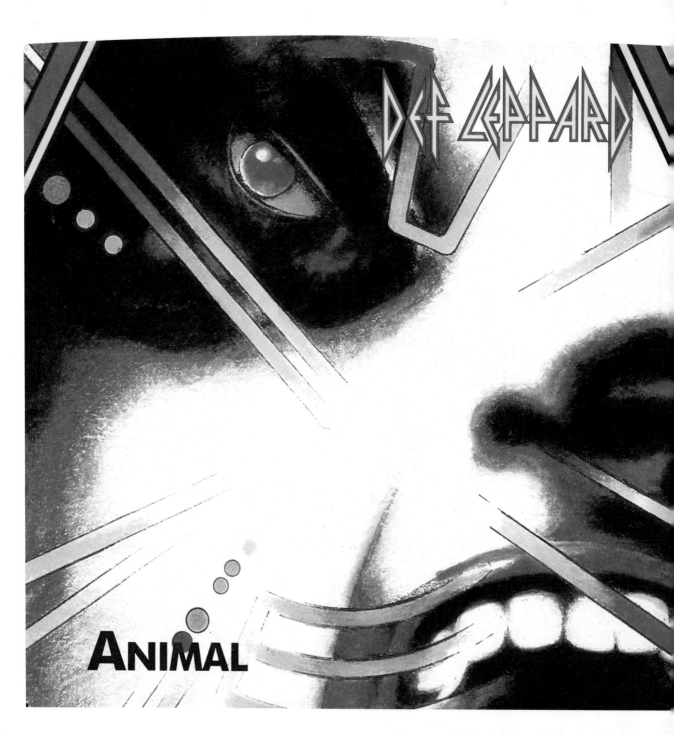

BOSTON

WE'RE READY

MCA-52985

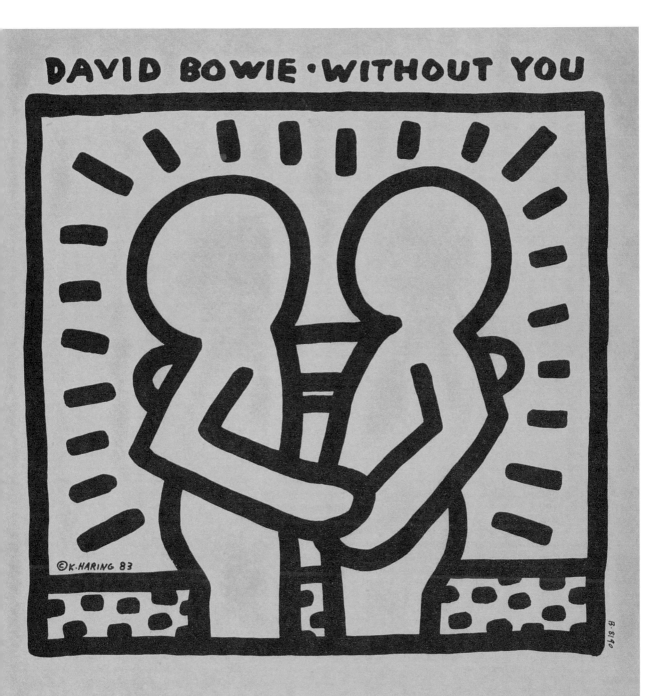

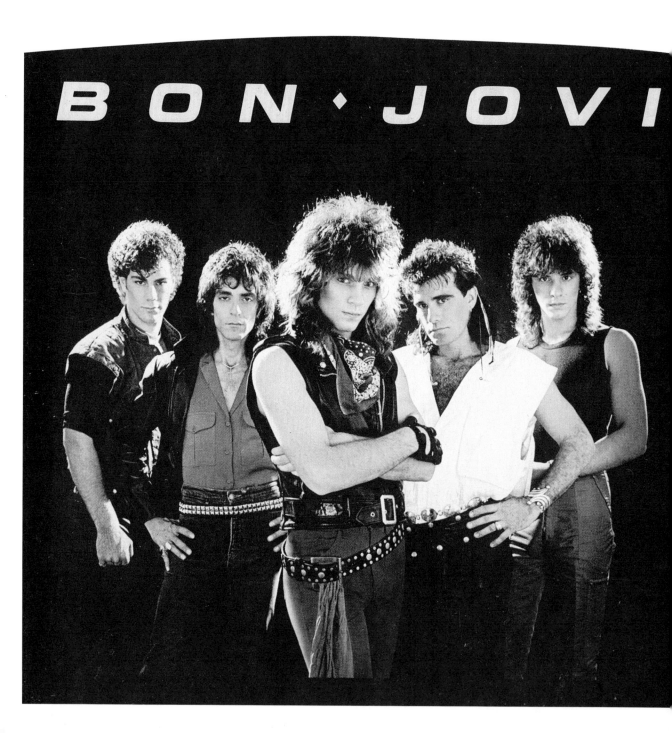

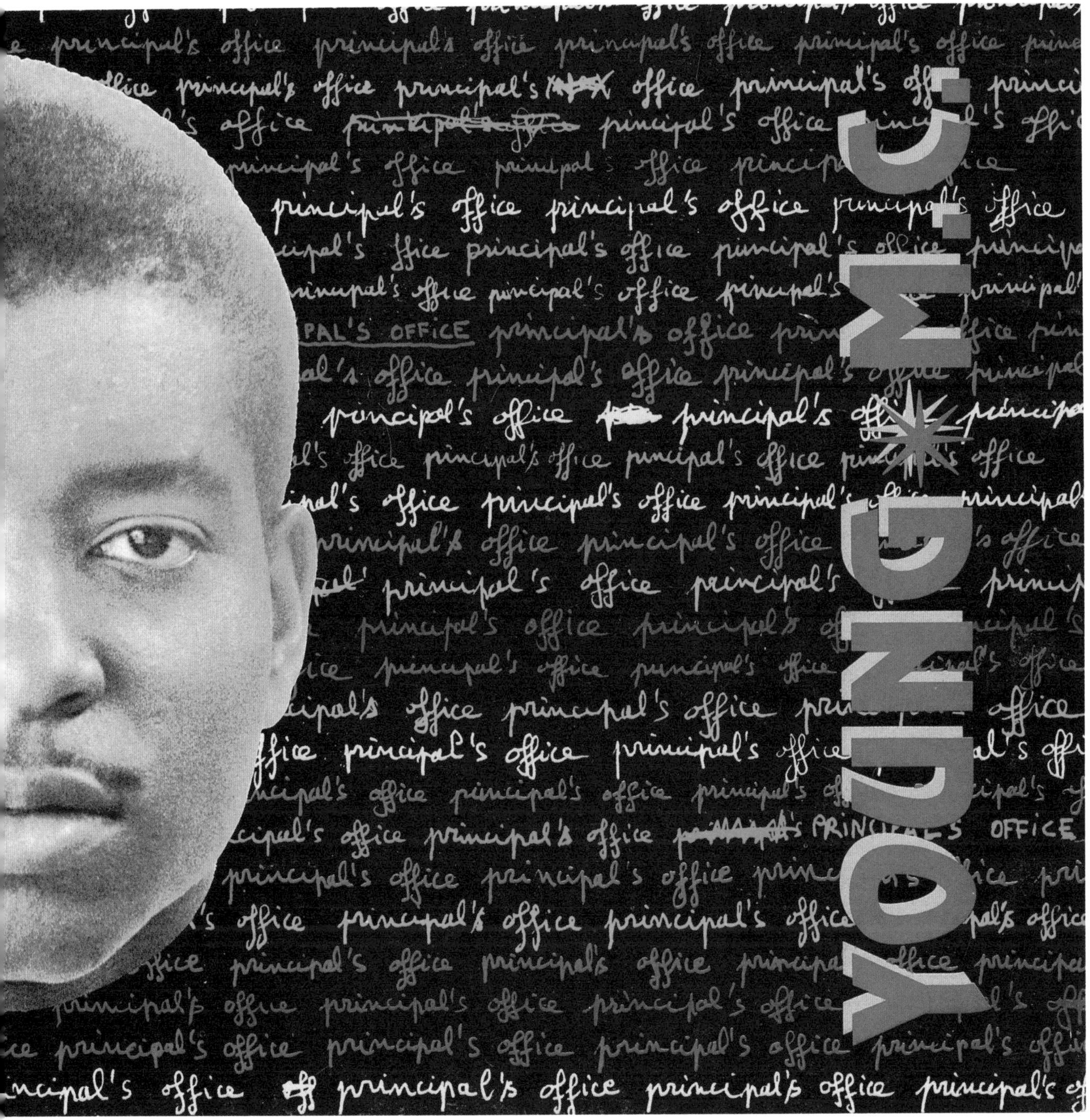

JASMINE MINKS

WHAT'S HAPPENING

23

Section 25 · Back To Wonder · Beating Heart · Fac 68

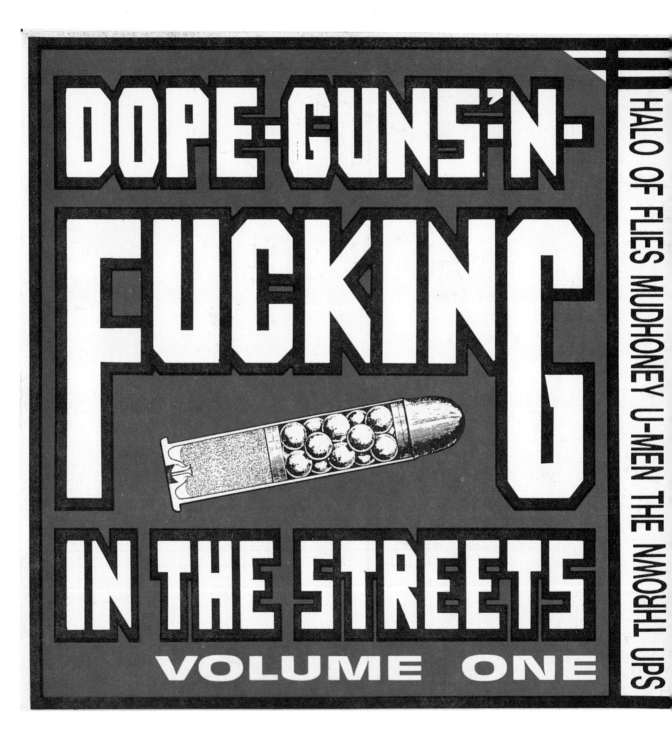

PRETENDERS

STOP YOUR SOBBING

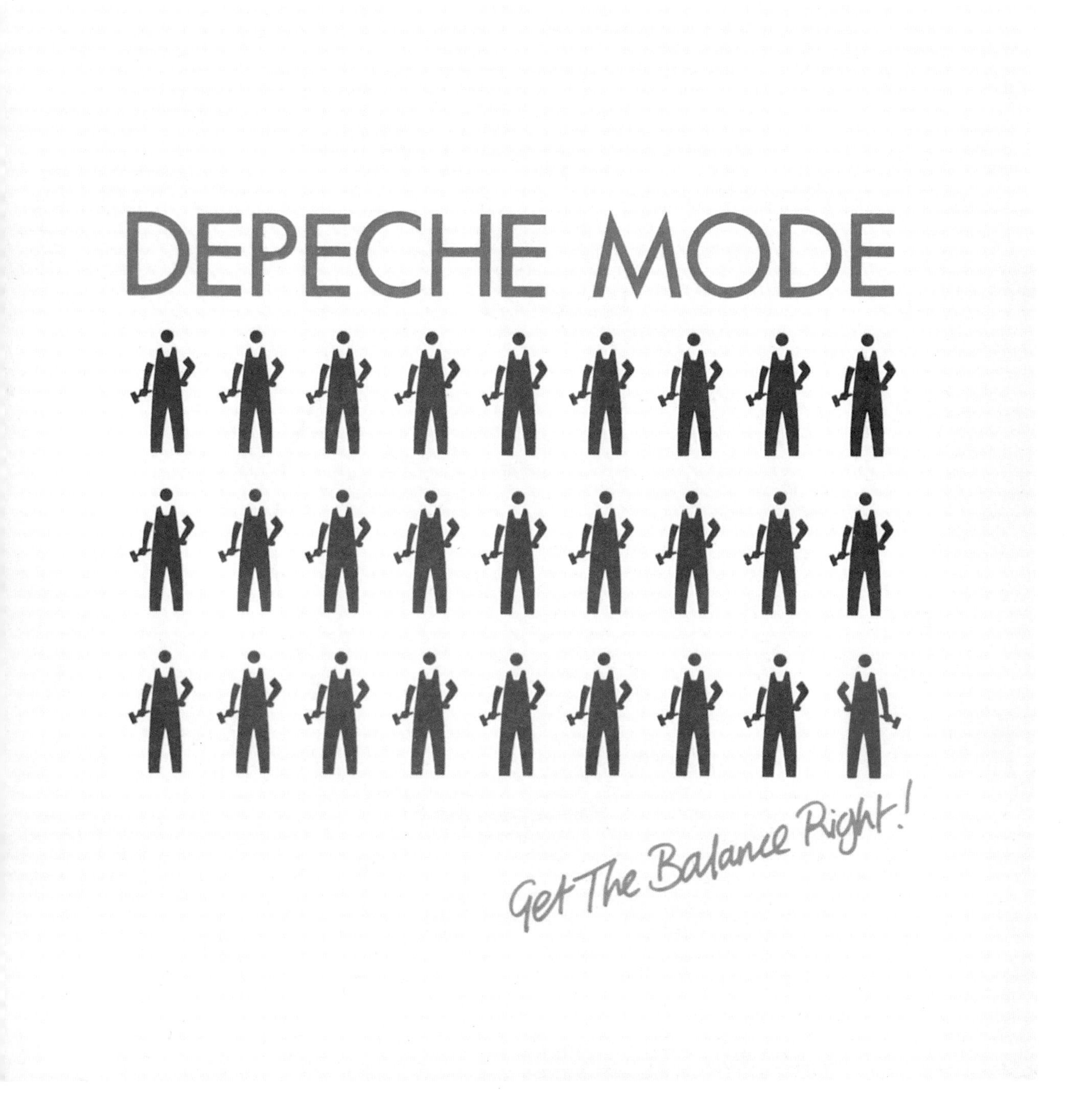
DEPECHE MODE
Get The Balance Right!

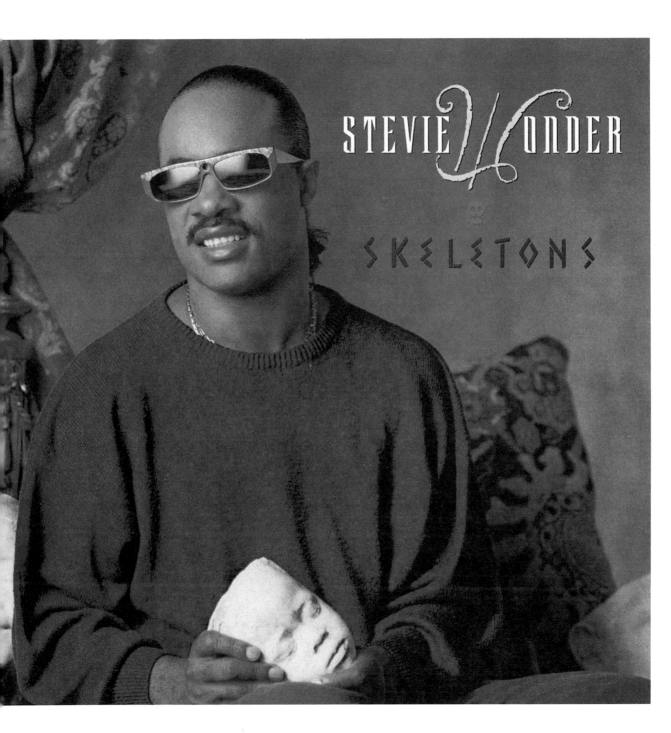

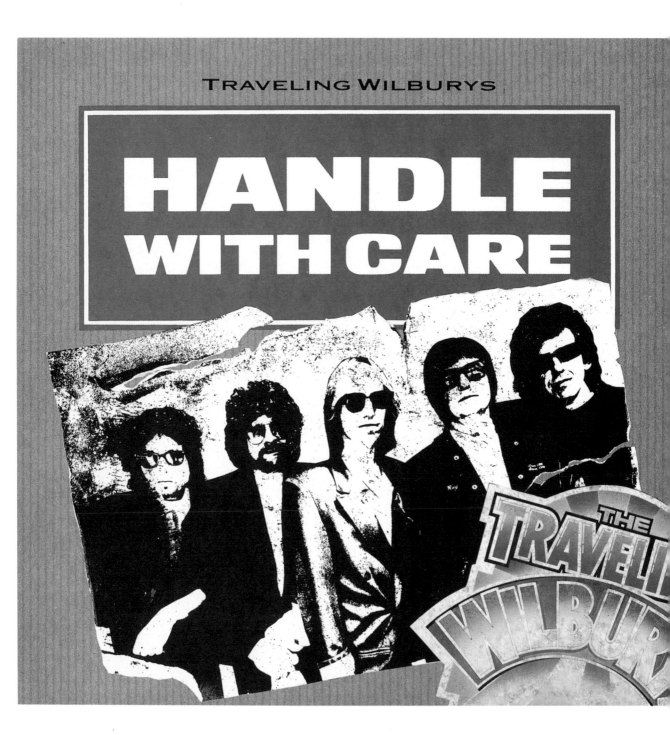

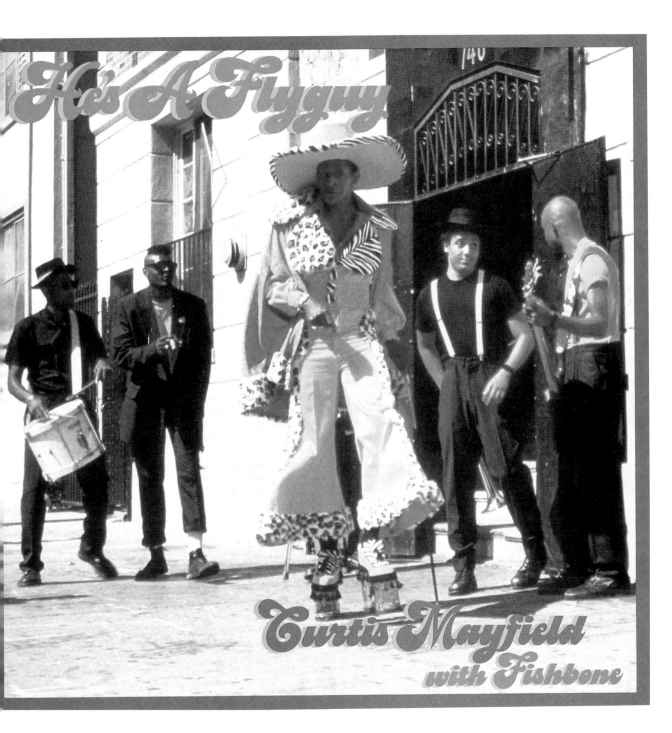

VINYL FETISH

1990

ART CHANTRY

The 1990s were the glory years of the independent 45, a time when this outmoded medium became the sole voice of a disenfranchised generation. All but abandoned as unprofitable by corporate record labels, the little 45 became an underground fetish object.

Like all histories bracketed in decades, the story of the 45 in the 1990s began in the preceding years. By the mid-1980s the commercial single was essentially dead. But aside from the cassette tape— an acoustically inferior medium—the 45 was the only affordable recording vehicle for the teeming underground culture kick-started by the punk movement in the 1970s. This culture festered in the 1980s, when the commercial onslaught of the compact disc wiped out the vinyl LP along with its bastard child, the 45.

Inspired by the legendary do-it-yourself record labels that spawned the early punk culture (labels like Cherry Red, and 2 Tone), a number of "subterranean" independents emerged in the late 1980s. Known as "indies," they were run by collectors, fans, and other music geeks and at first barely deserved the designation "labels." These groups, with names like Amphetamine Reptile, Dischord, K, Frontier, and Sympathy for the Record Industry, began churning out singles for their friends and comrades. More importantly, labels like Sub Pop and Estrus initiated the revolutionary "singles club" concept, where for a fixed annual fee a subscriber would receive a limited edition 45 in the mail at regular intervals. The singles clubs promoted the sponsoring labels, created steady profitable cash flow, built a band's audience, developed mailing lists of ready consumers, and, perhaps most importantly, whetted the appetites of a new group of obsessive collectors. They also opened a regular forum of exposure and experimentation for artists, designers, and cartoonists to display their peculiar talents unfettered by budgetary and marketing constraints. Together the people interested in this "scene" built a dialog that became the primary information source of those lost souls without access to any other sort of communication media. In other words, they built a community.

They also initiated an astonishing contest of creative one-upsmanship. Anything was conceptually possible; budgets consisted of whatever anybody could build with a few bucks and a few man-hours. A producer would come up with an idea, and then figure out how to execute it. Sleeves were photocopied, silkscreened, glued together, punched, hand drawn, bullet riddled, blood stained, torn, nailed, duct taped, die cut, potato stamped, origamied, bolted, sandpapered, and tarred. The most extreme example: a single buried in a soil-filled basket capped by a thatch of growing grass. You had to dig up the record.

Cover images were taken from anywhere and everywhere. There were dead babies, monsters driving hot rods, naked girls, psychedelia, surrealist images of all kinds, old advertising graphics, Peter Max prints—it was all fair game. Just about every prominent cartoonist or illustrator that has emerged over the last two decades has done a sleeve or two.

And it wasn't just the covers that were subject to relentless experimentation. The vinyl itself became a focus of obsessive creative activity. There were big holes, small holes, multiple holes, every conceivable color of plastic (opaque, transparent, glow-in-the-dark). There were wildly printed and strangely shaped labels, artwork and secret messages scratched into vinyl, odd shapes (square!), oversized records (8 inches!), undersized records (5 inches!), loops, images silkscreened on clear disks, artwork scratched onto smooth records (no music!), double grooves, and records that played "backward" from the inside out. If you can think of a gimmick, somebody tried it.

When some of the bands hit the big time (notably Nirvana), the floodgates opened, and 45s, once again, began to sell. All independent music was promoted with singles rather than tapes. Business interests took note. By the mid-1990s, there were literally thousands of "indie" singles being produced by everyone from obscure garage bands to multinational corporations. Creative quality dropped when the few pressing plants geared up for the increased volume and began to limit a designer's options. At the same time, print shops began raising prices for quick service, all due to the sudden glut of work.

The small labels found themselves being edged out of production schedules to make room for superstar bands trying to look "indie," and record shops were flooded with product they could no longer move. The music became formulaic and homogenized. Tastes changed, economies staggered, and it became cheaper to release your own self-published compact disc than your own 45.

In the last few years sales of singles have dwindled as independent labels have abandoned them or just gone out of business. Once again the medium appears doomed. But for most of the 1990s, the 45 had a truly glorious run.

ART CHANTRY, the subversive design genius behind countless independent 45s, is an underground legend in his own right and the subject of *Some People Can't Surf: The Graphic Design of Art Chantry* (Chronicle, 2001).

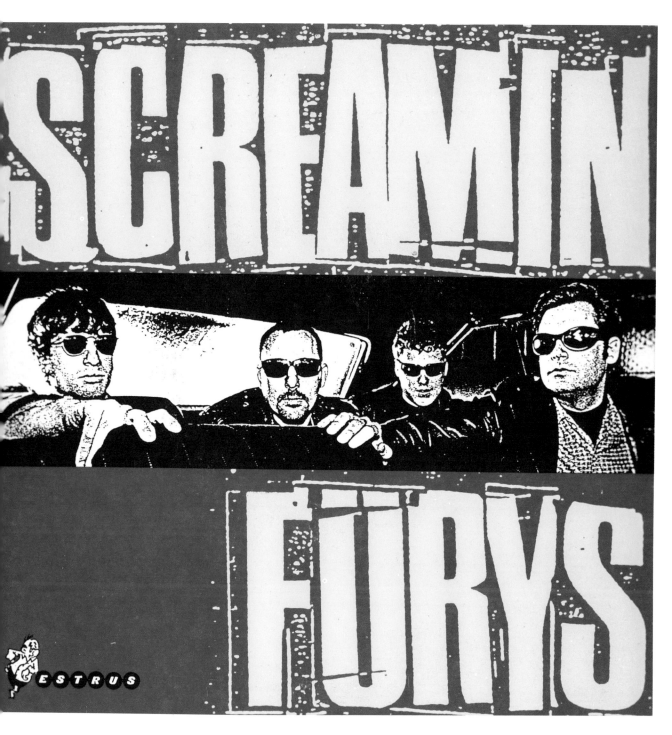

THE

MURDER CITY DEVILS

SUB POP

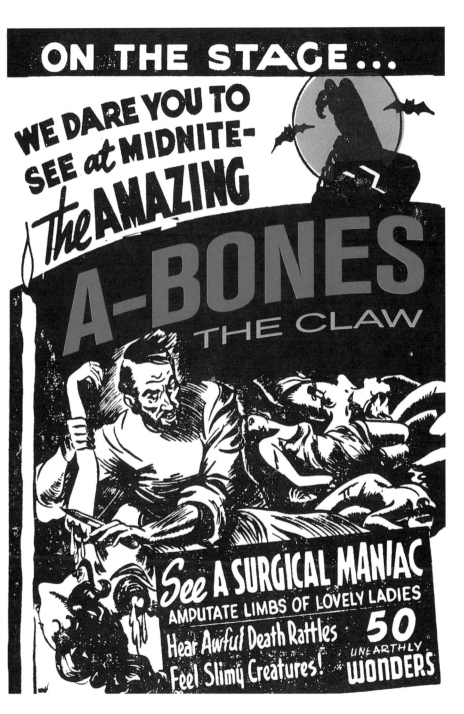

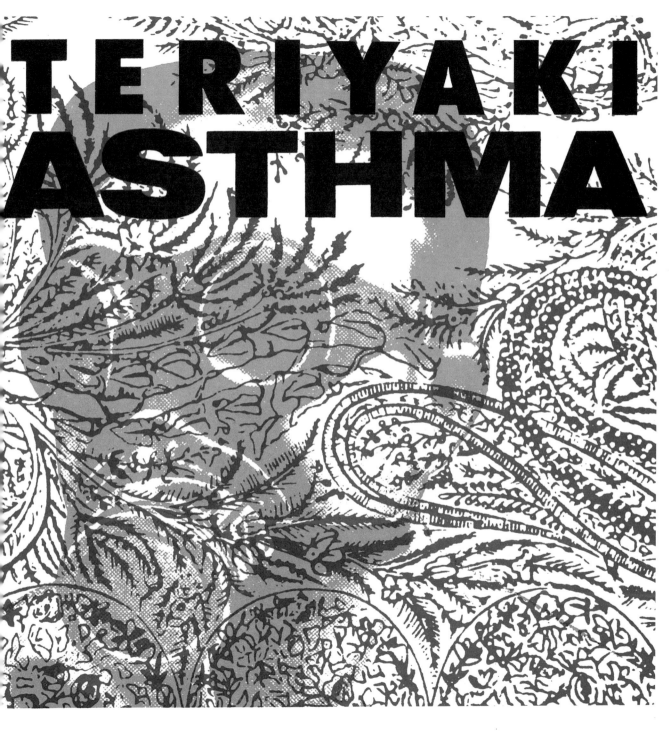

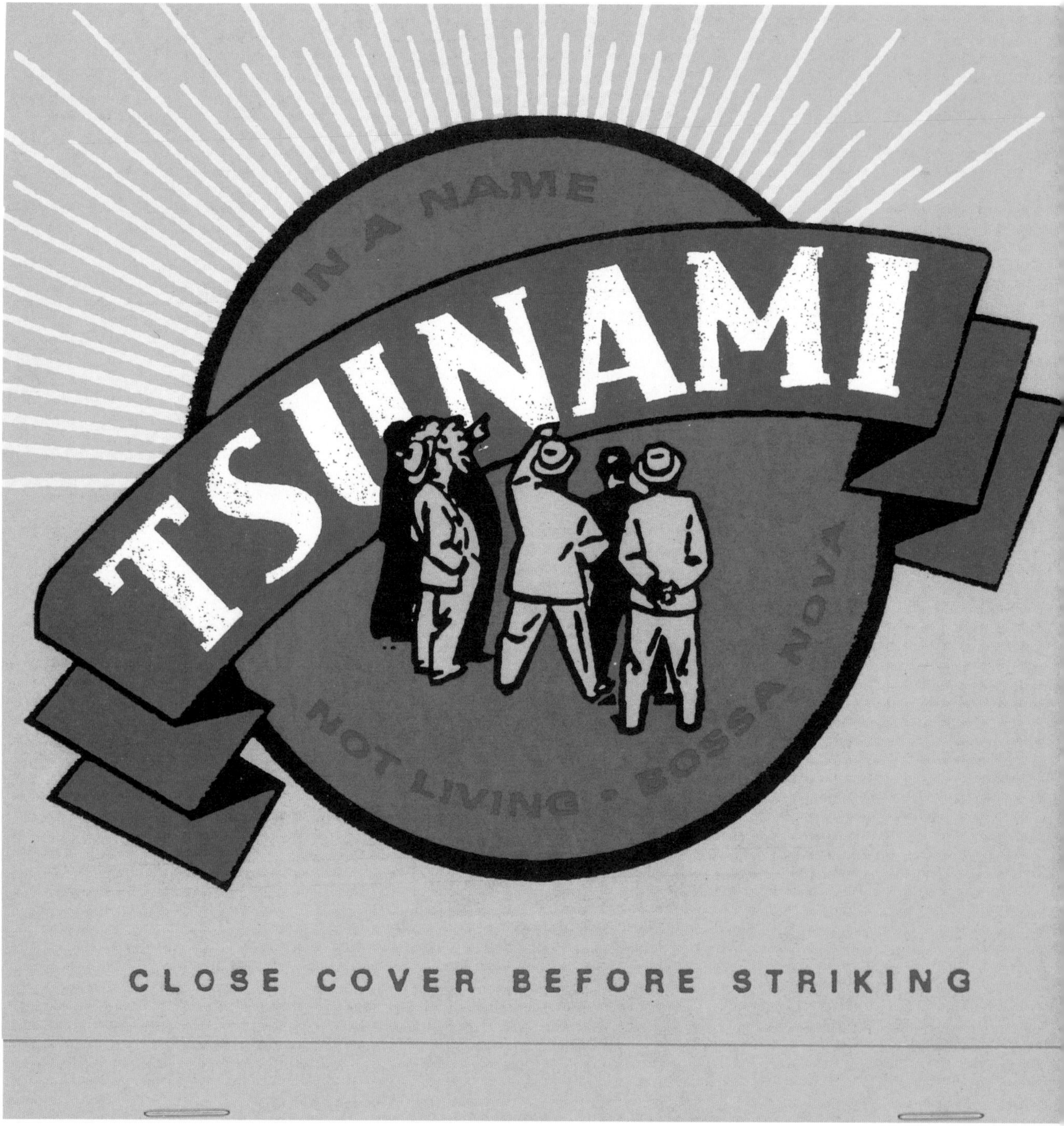

IN A NAME

TSUNAMI

NOT LIVING · BOSSA NOVA

CLOSE COVER BEFORE STRIKING

INSTANT SET

ORANGE

ARTIFICIAL FLAVOR

POLVO

❧ *Celebrate the New Dark Age* ❧

RECORDS

Produce of North Carolina

Net 5 OZ/ 142 g.

THE MURDER CITY DEVILS
"Christmas Bonus Single"

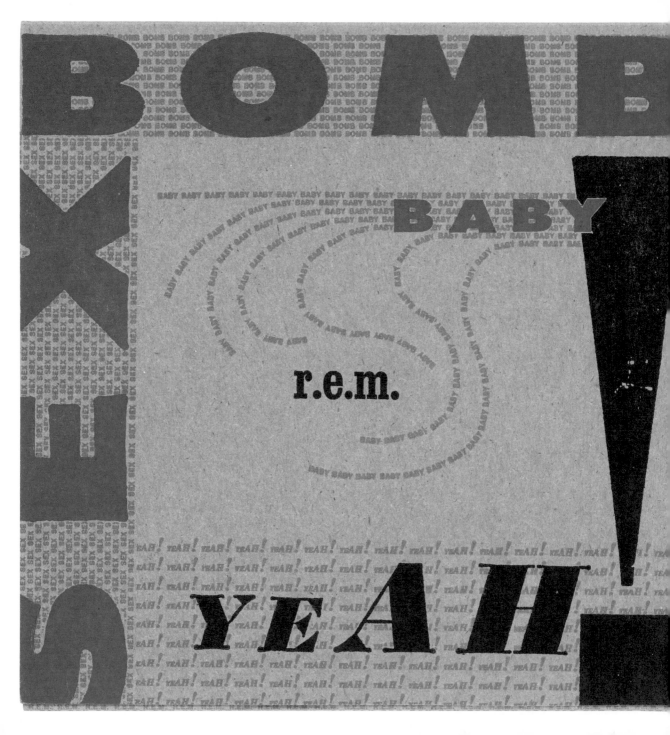

TUNISIE RF

POSTES

94f

L.DUMOULIN

PUYPLAS

Christmas in Tunisia

KRS 242

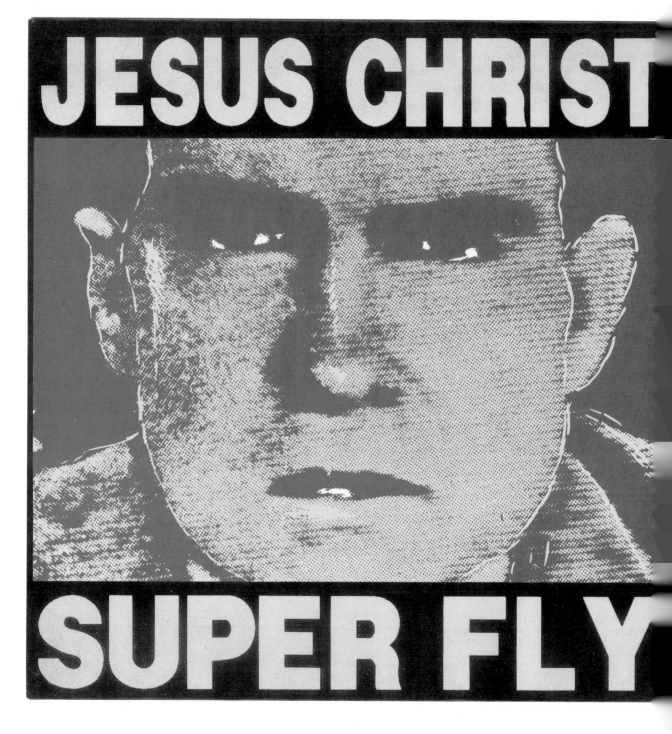

WHEN ANGELS SHED THEIR WINGS

devils head records number 06

VOLUME 2

one king down
SPILL THE BLOOD

BROTHER'S KEEPER
DEAD SKIN MASK

Ringo Starr ★ weight of the world

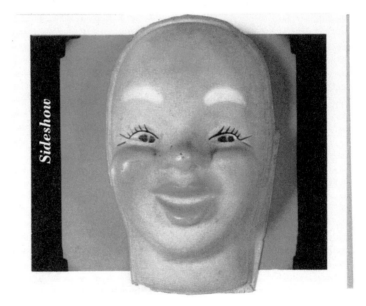

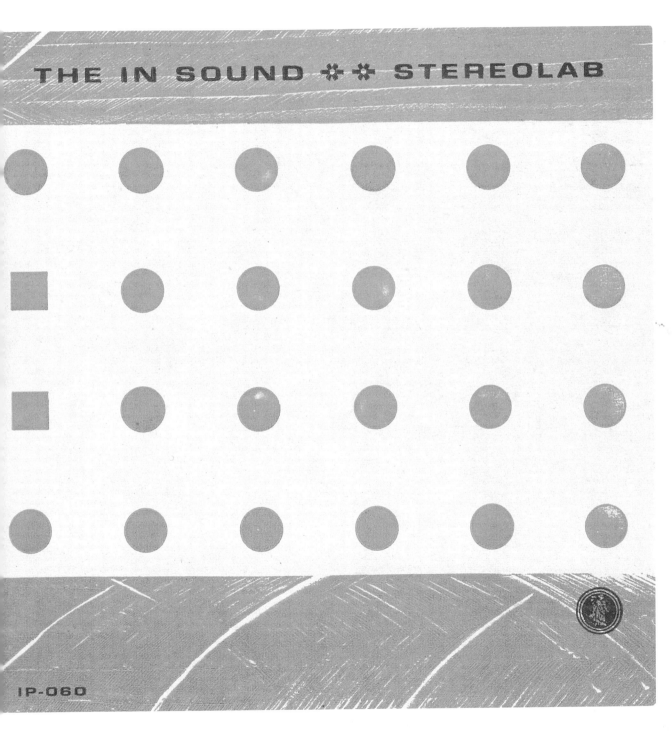

DISCOGRAPHY

The 1950s

Sammy Davis, Jr.
Here's Lookin' at You
Decca, 1956

Tony Bennett
Tony Bennett
Columbia, 1957

Duke Ellington
Uptown
Columbia, c. 1956

Fats Domino
Here Comes Fats
Imperial, 1957

Elvis Presley
King Creole
RCA Victor, c. 1959

Elvis Presley
A Touch of Gold
RCA Victor, 1959

Matt Dennis
Dennis, Anyone?
RCA Victor, c. 1957

Joni James
When I Fall in Love
MGM, c. 1957

Les Paul and Mary Ford
Sitting on Top of the World!
Capitol, 1955

Dean Martin
Sunny Italy
Capitol, 1953

Liberace
Liberace by Candlelight
Columbia, 1953

Nat King Cole
Unforgettable
Capitol, c. 1953

Perfect for Dancing/Rumbas
RCA Victor, 1955

Perfect for Dancing/Waltzes
RCA Victor, 1955

The Three Suns
Soft and Sweet
RCA Victor, 1955

Bobby Dukoff
Sax in Silk
RCA Victor, 1954

Benny Goodman
Walt Disney's 2 for the Record
Capitol, c. 1954

Boston Pops Orchestra
Slaughter on 10th Avenue
RCA Victor, c. 1952

The Philadelphia Orchestra
Symphonie Fantastique
Columbia, c. 1952

Rosemary Clooney
Rosemary Clooney
Columbia, 1957

Duke Ellington
Skin Deep/The Mooche
Columbia, c. 1954

Frank Sinatra
Frank Sinatra Sings Irving Berlin
Columbia, 1952

Frank Sinatra
Where Are You?
Capitol, 1957

Frank Sinatra
In the Wee Small Hours
Capitol, 1955

Frank Sinatra
3 Coins in the Fountain
Capitol, 1954

Frank Sinatra
Frank Sings Jerome Kern
Columbia, 1953

Frank Sinatra
Carousel
Columbia, 1953

Morton Gould
Blues by Gould
Columbia, c. 1954

Shorty Rogers & His Giants
Modern Sounds
Capitol, c. 1950

Al Cohn
Mr. Music
RCA Victor, 1954

Oscar Peterson
Oscar Peterson Plays Duke Ellington
Mercury, 1953
Illustrator: David Stone Martin

Stan Getz
Stan Getz Plays
Roost, 1951
Designer: Burt Goldblatt

Chet Baker
Chet Baker Plays
Pacific Jazz, c. 1953
Designer: John Brandt
Photographer: William Claxon

Ella Fitzgerald and
Louis Armstrong
Ella and Louis
Verve, 1956
Designer: Phil Stern

Tito Rodriguez
Mambo
RCA Victor, 1954

Xavier Cugat
Mambo at the Waldorf
Columbia, 1952

Ben Lights
Rhythm Rendezvous
Capitol, 1957

Jackie Gleason
Lonesome Echo
Capitol, 1955

Ricky Nelson
Ricky Nelson Sings
Imperial, 1957

Jerry Lee Lewis
Great Balls of Fire
Warner Brothers, 1957
Designer: Sun Records

American Society Concerts in the Home
Bell, 1959
Illustration: Pablo Picasso
Designer: Arthur Shimkin

American Society Concerts in the Home
Bell, 1959
Illustration: Pablo Picasso
Designer: Arthur Shimkin

The 1960s

Elvis Presley
Are You Lonesome To-night?
RCA Victor, 1960

Elvis Presley
A Big Hunk O' Love
RCA Victor, 1960

Bobby Rydell
The Best Man Cried
Cameo, 1962

Fabian
About This Thing Called Love
Chancellor, 1961

Chubby Checker
Loddy Lo
Parkway, 1963

Roy Orbison
Ride Away
MGM, 1965

The Everly Brothers
How Can I Meet Her
Warner Brothers, 1962

Paul Anka
Tonight, My Love, Tonight
ABC Paramount, 1961

The Dovells
Bristol Twistin' Annie
Parkway, 1961

The Beach Boys
Surfin' Safari
Capitol, 1962

The Beatles
She Loves You
Swan, 1964
Photographer: Dezo Hoffman

The Beatles
I'm Happy Just to Dance with You
Capitol, 1964
Photographer: Dezo Hoffman

The Beatles
Love Me Do
Capitol, 1962

The Beatles
We Can Work It Out/Day Tripper
Capitol, 1966

The Beatles
I Am the Walrus
Capitol, 1967

Plastic Ono Band
Give Peace a Chance
Apple, 1969

The Rolling Stones
Five by Five
Decca, 1964

The Rolling Stones
As Tears Go By
London, 1965

The Rolling Stones
Jumpin' Jack Flash
London, 1968
Photographer: David Bailey

The Rolling Stones
She's a Rainbow
London, 1967

The Impressions
Fool for You
Buddha, 1968

The Temptations
My Girl
Gordy, 1964

Simon & Garfunkel
The Boxer/Baby Driver
Columbia, 1968
[front & back]

Country Joe and The Fish
Who am I
Vanguard, 1968

The Majorettes
White Levi's
Troy, 1962

Sam the Sham and the Pharaohs
Ju Ju Hand
MGM, 1965

The Move
Blackberry Way
Polydor, c. 1969

The Buckinghams
Hey Baby (They're Playing Our Song)
Columbia, 1967

Manfred Mann
Sha La La
Ascot, 1964

The Young Rascals
Groovin'
Atlantic, 1967
Photographer: Russell Beal

The Yardbirds
Happenings Ten Years Time Ago
Epic, 1966

Blue Cheer
Summertime Blues
Philips, 1968

Donovan
Sunshine Superman
Epic, 1966

Simon & Garfunkel
Simon & Garfunkel at the Zoo
Columbia, 1968
Illustrator: Chas B. Slackman

Santana
Oye Como Va
Columbia, 1969

Tom Jones
She's a Lady
London, 1965

Patrick MacNee & Honor Blackman
Kinky Boots
Decca, 1964

The 1970s

Chicago
Baby, What a Big Surprise
Columbia, 1977

Chicago
Dialogue
Columbia, 1972

The Rolling Stones
Promotional compilation
Rolling Stones, 1977

The Beatles
Let it Be
Apple, 1970

Don McLean
American Pie
United Artist, 1971

America
Ventura Highway
Warner Brothers, 1972

George Harrison
Bangla Desh
Apple, 1971

T. Rex
Celebrate Summer
EMI, 1977

Gerry Rafferty
Night Owl
United Artists, 1979

Cat Stevens
Oh Very Young
A&M, 1974

The Romantics
What I Like About You
Nemperor, 1979

Rod Stewart
Do Ya Think I'm Sexy?
Warner Brothers, 1978

The Foundations
Build Me Up Buttercup
PYE, 1970

The Shirts
Out on the Ropes
Harvest, 1979

Eric Burdon & War
Spill The Wine
MGM, 1979

War
Why Can't We Be Friends?
United Artists, 1975

Sex Pistols
Anarchy in the U.K
Sex Pistols, 1977
Designer: Jamie Reed

Sex Pistols
Pretty Vacant
Warner Brothers, 1977
Designer: Jamie Reed

Sex Pistols
God Save the Queen
Virgin, 1977
Designer: Jamie Reed

The Rolling Stones
Shattered
Rolling Stones, 1978

Public Image LTD
Public Image/The Cowboy Song
Virgin, 1978
Photographer: Dennis Morris

Squeeze
Goodbye Girl
A&M, 1978

Alice Cooper
Schools Out/Gutter Cat
Warner Brothers, 1972

The Clash
White Riot
CBS, 1977

999
Emergency
U.A., 1978
Designer: Snow-George

Buzzcocks
Orgasm Addict
United Artist, 1977
Photographer: K. Cummins

D.O.A.
Wrong, 1978
Photographer and Designer:
Dane Simoes

Echo and the Bunnymen
The Pictures on the Wall
Zoo, 1979

The Misfists
Bullet
Plan-9, 1978

The Adverts
One Chord
Stiff, 1978

Motörhead
Ace of Spades
Bronze, c. 1979

A Band
No Love/Lowly Worm
Nancy, 1979
Designer: Matt Mullican

Talking Heads
Take Me to the River
Sire, 1978
Designer: Talking
Heads/Spencer Drate

The Monochrome Set
Alphaville/He's Frank
Rough Trade, 1979

Ramones
Rock 'N' Roll High School
Sire, 1979
Designer: Spencer Drate

Iggy Pop and The Stooges
I Got a Right
Siamese, 1973
Photographer and Designer:
Philippe Mogane/Mary Savage

Billy Preston
Space Race
A&M, 1972

Curtis Mayfield
Super Fly
Curtom, 1972

Grand Funk
Shinin' On
Capitol, 1974
Photographer: Lynn Goldsmith

Devo
Be Stiff
Stiff, 1978

Jimmy Cliff
The Harder They Come
Dynamic Sounds, 1972

Al Green
I'm Still in Love With You
London, 1972

The 1980s
John Lennon
(Just Like) Starting Over
Lenono Music, 1980

John Lennon
Watching the Wheels
Geffen , 1980
Photographer: Paul Goresh

Joan Jett and the Blackhearts
Fake Friends
MCA, 1983
Photographer: Dieter Zill
Designers: Spencer Drate and
Judith Salavetz

Bryan Adams
Straight from the Heart
A&M, 1983

The Rolling Stones
She's So Cold
Rolling Stones, 1980

The Rolling Stones
Terrifying
Rolling Stones, 1989

The Rolling Stones
Start Me Up
Rolling Stones, 1986

The Rolling Stones
One Hit (To The Body)
Rolling Stones, 1986

Aretha Franklin
Freeway of Love
Arista, 1985

Kiss
Tears Are Falling
Polygram, 1985

Def Leppard
Animal
Mercury, 1987
Photographer: Robert Erdman
Illustrator and designer: Satori

Boston
We're Ready
MCA, 1986
Illustrator: Roger Huyssen

The Cult
Wild Flower
Beggars Banquet, 1987
Photographer: David Skernick
Illustrator: Rick Griffin

It Bites
Still Too Young to Remember
Virgin, 1989
Designer: Roger Dean

The Kinks
Do it Again
Arista, 1985

David Bowie
Without You
EMI, 1983
Illustrator: Keith Haring

Debbie Harry
French Kiss
Geffen, 1986
Illustrator: Andy Warhol
Designer: Stephen Sprouse

Pat Benatar
Invincible
Chrysalis, 1985

Bon Jovi
Runaway
Polygram Records, 1984
Photographer: Geoffrey Thomas
Designer: Spencer Drate/Judith
Salavetz

B-52's
Rock Lobster
Island, 1980

Talking Heads
Cities
Sire, 1980
Illustrator: Plastics
Designer: Talking
Heads/Spencer Drate

Supertramp
Cannonball
A&M, 1985
Designer: Norman Moore

Blurt
The Fish Needs a Bike
Armageddon, 1981

Attention
Zero Hour
MB3, 1983

Visions
It's a Choice
Polygram, 1988
Designer: Spencer Drate/Judith
Salavetz

Young M.C.
Principal's Office
Island, 1989
Photographer and designer:
Salomon

Halo of Flies
No Time
Amphetamine Reptile, 1988
Designer: Haze

U-Men
Solid Action
Black Label, 1987

Jasmine Minks
What's Happening
Creation Records, 1985
Designer: Chromatone

Scars
Love Song
PRE, 1980
Designer: Bruce Licher

The Kinks
Good Day
Arista, 1984

Artery
Cars in Motion
Aardvark, 1981
Designer: Graham Gaunx

Neef
23
Independent Project, 1980
Designer: Bruce Licher

Section 25
Back to Wonder
Factory, 1982

Halo of Flies et. al.
*Dope-Guns'-N-Fucking in the
Streets (Vol. I)*
Amphetamine Reptile, 1987
Designer: D. Deuteronomy

Thug
Dad/Thug
Black Eye, 1987

Pretenders
Stop Your Sobbing
Real, 1980
Designer: Spencer Drate

Depeche Mode
Get the Balance Right!
Mute, 1989

Wham!
Freedom
Columbia, 1985

Stevie Wonder
Skeletons
Motown, 1987

The Traveling Wilburys
Handle with Care
Wilbury, 1988
Photographer: Neal Preston
Designer: Wherefore Art

Curtis Mayfield with Fishbone
He's a Flyguy
Arista, 1988

The 1990s

Death Valley
Apollo XIII
D.Valley/Estrus, 1996
Designer: Art Chantry

Jack O' Fire
Punkin'
Estrus, 1994
Designer: Art Chantry

Man . . . or Astro-man?
World Out of Mind
Estrus, 1994
Designer: Art Chantry

The Mummies et. al.
Fuck You Spaceman!
Planet Pimp, 1996

Skullflower
Ponyland
Sympathy for the Record
Industry, 1997
Illustrator: Larry Welz

7 Year Bitch
Miss Understood
Man's Ruin, 1996
Illustrator/designer: Frank Kozik

Teengenerate
Teengenerate
Dionysus, 1994

Dale Crover
Drumb
Man's Ruin, 1996
Illustrator/designer: Frank Kozik

Cheap Trick
Baby Talk/Brontosaurus
Sub Pop, 1997

The Yo-Yo's
Time of Your Life
Sub Pop, 2000
Illustrator: Charles Burns

The Stool Pigeons
I'm The One
Sympathy for the Record
Industry, 1998

Tree
Smash the State!
Man's Ruin, 1996
Illustrator/designer: Frank Kozik

Electric Frankenstein
Your So Fake/Rocket in My Pocket
Estrus, 1998
Designer: Art Chantry

Screamin' Furys
Why
Estrus, 1997
Photographer: Charles Gullung
Designer: Art Chantry

Von Ryan's Express
Ghetto Pose
Sub Pop, 1994
Designer: Jeff Kleinsmith

The Murder City Devils
Gluecifer
Sub Pop, 1999
Designer: Jeff Kleinsmith

Hellacopters
Looking at Me
Estrus, 1998
Designer: Art Chantry

The A-Bones
Spooks-A-Poppin' Theme
Norton, 1993

Cows
Slap Black
Amphetamine Reptile, 1990
Designer: Haze XXL

Artist complication (featuring Nirvana)
Teriyaki Asthma
C/Z, 1990
Designer: Art Chantry

The Spitfires
Cut Me Some Slack
Estrus, 1999
Designer: Art Chantry

Fatal Flying Guilloteens
Shake Train
Estrus, 1999
Designer: Art Chantry

Tsunami
In a Name
Simple Machines, 1993
Designers: Steve Reskinans and John Palmer

The Volcanos
Deora/Drums Fell Off a Cliff
Estrus, 1996
Designer: Art Chantry

The Cramps
How Come You Do Me?/Let Get Fucked Up
Giant, 1994

The Del Lagunas
Time Tunnel
Estrus, 1995
Designer: Art Chantry

Polvo
Celebrate the New Dark Age
Merge, 1994
Designer: Bruce Licher

The Amazing Crowns
Chop Shop/Amateur Night
Sub Pop, 1999
Designer: Jeff Kleinsmith

Crooked Fingers
Atchafalayan Death Waltz
Sub Pop, 1999

The Murder City Devils
Christmas Bonus Single
Jeff and Amy's Paper Bag
Series, 1998
Designer: Jeff Kleinsmith

R.E.M.
Sex Bomb
R.E.M/Athens, 1994
Designer: Bruce Licher
[front and back]

Godheadsilo
Elephantitus of the Night
Kill Rock Stars, 1994

The Switch Trout
Sonic Masters
Estrus, 1999
Designer: Art Chantry

Velocity Girl
Nothing
Sub Pop, 1996
Designer: Jeff Kleinsmith

The Wildebeests
One+One/Teenage Love/Gorilla Got Me
Sympathy for the Record
Industry, 1999

Jesus Christ Super Fly
Big Shit/Rocket Scientist
Rise, 1992
Designer: Frank Kozik

When Angels Shed Their Wings
Volume II
Devils Head, 1990

Madam X
*Funnel of Love/Lover
Man/Scotch Soda*
Estrus, 1996
Photographer: A. Aubry
Designer: Art Chantry

Worst Case Scenario
Worst Case Scenario
Look Out , 1995

Ringo Starr
Weight of the World
Private Music, 1992

Sideshow
Samp Sunnyside
Caulfield, 1994
Designer: Jeff Kleinsmith

Helmet
In the Meantime
Amphetamine Reptile, 1992
Designer: Haze Graphics

Tears for Fears
Advice for the Young at Heart
Phonogram, 1990
Photographer: David
Scheinman/Avid Images
Designer: Stylorouge

Migala
North of Fire
Sub Pop, 2000
Designer: Jeff Kleinsmith

Stereolab
The In Sound
Independent Project, 1998
Designer: Bruce Licher

ACKNOWLEDGMENTS

The publishers: Kevin Lippert, Mark Lamster, Deb Wood, and the staff at Princeton Architectural Press believed that this important part of music culture warranted publication in book form.

The collectors: Bruce Alexander, Stuart A. Goldman, Chuck Granata, Steven Turner, Mark Arm, Bruce Licher, Jeff Kleinsmith (Subpop), Long Gone John (Sympathy Records), Billy (Norton Records), Tom Hazelmyer (Reptile Records), Frank Kozik, Art Chantry, Nick Miraglia, Tara and Jason. Thank you for making the book happen.

The writers: Chuck Granata, Eric Kohler, Roger Dean, Bob Grossweiner, Art Chantry. Thank you for your insight into this unheralded medium.

The inspiration: Roger Dean, John Lennon, The Stones, Jütka Salavetz, Justin and Ariel, Doo Wop, my first Elvis single, WCBS-FM, Sire and Seymour Stein, Kenny and Meryl Laguna, Joan Jett, Jon Bon Jovi, Talking Heads, U2, my first AC/DC record, Led Zeppelin, Bernard Stollman, John Berg, and all those fantastic 45s.

The author acknowledges the assistance and support of the following record labels who have generously allowed their singles to be reproduced in the volume: A&M Records, Aardvark, ABC Paramount, Amphetamine Reptile Records, Apple Records, Arista Records, Armageddon Record, Ascot Records, ATCO, Atlantic Records, Beggars Banquet, Black Eye, Black Label Records, Black Records, Bronze Records LTD, Buddha Records, C/Z Records, Cameo, Capitol Records, Caulfield Records, CBS Records, Chancellor, Chrysalis, Columbia Records, Curtom Records, D. Valley, Dionysus Records, Dynamic Sounds Recordings, EMI America Record, Emperor Jones, Epic Records, Estrus Records, Geffen Records, Giant Records, Gordy, Harvest, Imperial Records, Caulfield Records, Independent Project Records, Island Records, Jeff and Amy's Paper Bag Series Records, Kill Rock Stars, Lenono Music, Liberty Records, London Records, Look Out Records, Man's Ruin Records, MCA Records, Mercury Records, Merge Records, MGM Records, Motown Records, Mute Records, Nancy Records, Nemperor Records, Norton Records, Parkway Records, Philips, Phonogram Ltd., Plan-9, Planet Pimp Records, Polygram Records, PRE, Private Music, PYE Records, R.E.M/Athens Ltd., Radarscope Records, RCA Victor, Real Records, Rise Records, Rolling Stones Records, Roost Records, Roswell Records, Rough Trade Records, Sex Pistols Records, Siamese Records, Simple Machines Records, Sire Records, Stiff Records, Sub Pop Records, Swan, Sympathy For the Record Industry, The Decca Record Company, Troy Records, United Artists Records, Vangard Records, Verve Records, Virgin Records, Warner Brothers, Wilbury, Wrong Records.